gluten-free
Family Favorites

Susan Cornelius Hinderaker

Photographs by Andrew Hinderaker

WIMMER
COOKBOOKS

A CONSOLIDATED GRAPHICS COMPANY

800.548.2537 wimmerco.com

The purpose of this book is to provide a resource to those with Celiac Disease or gluten intolerance who want to offer great tasting meals to their entire family. All proceeds from the sale of *Gluten-Free Family Favorites* go to support the University of Chicago Celiac Disease Program.

First Edition

First Printing   October 2005   500 copies

ISBN 0-9773899-0-1

Copies of *Gluten-Free Family Favorites* may be obtained by sending $19.95, plus $6.05 shipping and handling to the following address. North Carolina residents should add $1.50 sales tax.

Susan Cornelius Hinderaker
6068 Foggy Glen Place
Weddington, NC 28104
(704) 975-8794
celiackids@carolina.rr.com

for James, Andrew, and Mark

Acknowledgments

When my children were diagnosed with Celiac Disease in 2001, I began putting together this cookbook. I would like to express my gratitude to those who offered inspiration and encouragement:

Anne, the first person who ever mentioned the words "gluten intolerance" to me and who shared many of her favorite recipes.

Mrs. Phyllis Brogden and the "Food Chain Gang" of the Philadelphia Celiac Support Group and the Delphi Celiac Disease Online Support Group for wonderful guidance on the gluten-free diet and gluten-free products.

My friend Allyson, who passed on advice from the owner of her favorite Chinese restaurant, "No substitution, just leave it out!"

Claudia, who enthusiastically encouraged me to publish my cookbook.

My family, James, Andrew, and Mark for trying new recipes, providing feedback, and doing mounds of dishes.

Andrew, who often had to take pictures of his food before he could eat it.

My family and friends who shared their favorite recipes with me especially Mom, Karen, Eula, Carrie, Sandi, Anne, Debbie, and Terri.

Karen, James, Mark, Andrew, and Mom for reading the recipes and making editorial comments. This is truly a family effort and I enjoyed working with everyone to make it happen.

Susan Cornelius Hinderaker

Contents

Introduction

A gluten-free diet is necessary for those with Celiac Disease who must eliminate wheat, oats, rye, and barley from their diet. Although preparing gluten-free meals may seem a little daunting at first, you may find, as we did, that eating at home more frequently has advantages such as improving family time and allowing you to eat healthier, more varied foods. We hope this cookbook will help make your meal planning more fun and that you will enjoy sharing these dishes with your family and friends.

The recipes in this book have been developed for the entire family to enjoy, not just those on a gluten-free diet. The recipes have been tested by our entire family. Our preference is for foods that can be made with every day ingredients supplemented when necessary with specialty foods from gluten-free food suppliers. Many of the ingredients needed to prepare these recipes can be found at your supermarket or natural foods store.

Our recipes for baking rely more heavily on special ingredients that may be purchased at a natural foods store or by mail order. Rather than purchasing an array of flours for the pantry, we prefer to use premixed flours that already include a leavening agent. These products offer convenience and freshness especially for those who do not bake often.

Staying gluten-free requires frequent communication with food manufacturers to determine the gluten-free status of each product. Because of this, many Celiacs are brand loyal and prefer to stick with a known product rather than research a new one. Our personal preference is to use the products of companies who have made our diet easier by identifying all sources of gluten on their labels or by providing the gluten-free status of their products on their company website. We have included brand names of products known to be gluten-free at the time of publication. Each person on the gluten-free diet must keep themselves up-to-date on all ingredients and products consumed by contacting the manufacturer on a regular basis.

Each recipe section begins with a color photograph to illustrate the wonderful foods you can make from our collection of gluten-free recipes. Whether you are just starting on a gluten-free diet, or are experienced with the diet and want to add variety to your daily meals, we hope you will enjoy the cookbook.

Please contact the manufacturer to confirm the gluten-free status of all products. Companies change ingredient frequently so it is important to review the ingredient list of all products each time you purchase them.

Appetizers, Snacks & Beverages

Appetizers, Snacks & Beverages

Shrimp Scampi

2   tablespoons extra virgin olive oil
2   tablespoons dry white wine
6   cloves garlic, minced or pressed
¼   teaspoon McCormick paprika
    Salt and freshly ground black pepper

1   tablespoon McCormick parsley
    flakes
24 large shrimp (about 1 pound) peeled
    and deveined, with tails
2   medium lemons, halved, for garnish

In a bowl, combine oil, wine, garlic, paprika, salt, pepper, and parsley. Add shrimp and toss well in marinade. Refrigerate, covered, for 1 hour. Thread 6 shrimp crosswise on each of 4 skewers. Broil 3 inches from high heat, brushing with marinade. Broil until cooked through, 2 to 3 minutes, turning once. Remove shrimp to a large platter and serve with lemon halves alongside.

Serves 4

Mini Goat Cheese Tarts

1 cup finely ground walnuts

2 tablespoons unsalted butter, melted

1 teaspoon salt, divided

Freshly ground black pepper

8 ounces Philadelphia cream cheese, softened

10 ounces goat cheese

2 large eggs, lightly beaten

2 tablespoons chopped fresh chives

1 tablespoon red bell pepper, finely chopped

9 walnut halves, for garnish

Preheat the oven to 350°. Butter 36 nonstick mini-muffin cups. In a medium bowl, combine the ground walnuts, butter, and ½ teaspoon salt. Season with freshly ground black pepper. Stir until combined. Spoon a teaspoon of the walnut mixture into each cup and press down into the bottom of the cups.

With an electric mixer, beat the cream cheese until light and fluffy. Add the goat cheese and beat until creamy. Add the eggs and beat until well combined. Add the chives, the remaining ½ teaspoon salt, and freshly ground black pepper. Divide the goat cheese mixture between the cups and smooth the tops. Set a walnut piece on top of half of the mini tarts. Top the remaining mini tarts with the chopped red peppers. Bake until puffed, about 15 minutes. Let the mini tarts cool on a rack for 5 minutes, then remove from muffin cups using a small rubber spatula. Serve warm.

Serves 12

Hoisin and Plum Sauce Chicken Wings

5 pounds fresh chicken wings

1½ cups San-J Tamari wheat free soy sauce

3 cups Holland House sherry cooking wine

1 cup Premier Japan Organic wheat-free hoisin sauce

¾ cup Thai Kitchen light sweet plum sauce

¾ cup Heinz apple cider vinegar

½ cup honey

18 green onions, minced

6 garlic cloves, minced or pressed

In a medium saucepan, combine all the ingredients except chicken wings. Bring to a boil over medium heat. Reduce heat and simmer the sauce for 5 minutes. Remove from heat and cool to room temperature. Place the chicken wings in a 2-gallon Ziploc Freezer Bag. Pour the cooled marinade over the wings. Refrigerate overnight.

Preheat oven to 375°. Oil a large roasting pan. Drain the chicken wings, reserving the marinade. Boil the marinade for 5 minutes. Roast the wings for 1 to 1½ hours, basting every 20 minutes with the reserved marinade and turning the wings occasionally to brown evenly. Remove the wings from pan and cool on large sheets of foil. When cool, the wings may be wrapped and stored in the refrigerator up to 3 days. Serve the wings warm or at room temperature.

Serves 12

Bake at 325° if using a dark, nonstick roasting pan. The hoisin sauce is available from Miss Roben's (800) 891-0083 or www.allergygrocer.com. Please contact Epicurean International (510) 675-9025 for a list of gluten-free Thai Kitchen products.

Tangy Chicken Wings

7½ pounds Tyson chicken wing sections
1 cup fresh lime juice (from 8 to 10 limes)
1 cup apricot preserves (such as Smucker's Apricot Preserves)
1 cup San-J Tamari wheat free soy sauce

⅔ cup sugar
4 large garlic cloves
2 large disposable foil roasting pans (about 16 x 20)

Preheat oven to 425°. Divide wings between 2 large roasting pans, arranging in single layers. Purée remaining ingredients in a blender and pour mixture over wings, dividing evenly between pans. Bake wings in upper and lower thirds of oven 40 minutes. Turn wings over and switch position of pans in oven, then bake about 35 minutes more, or until liquid is thick and sticky. Serve wings warm or at room temperature.

Serves 20

Tyson Chicken Wings can be found in the frozen foods section of the store. The UPC# is 23700 16223.

Buffalo Chicken Wings

1   **bottle Mr. Spice Hot Wing! Sauce**   4   **pounds fresh chicken wings**

Preheat oven to 500°. Arrange chicken wings in a 13 x 9-inch glass baking dish. Drizzle sauce over wings. Cook in oven 40 minutes. When done, brush with additional sauce. Mix until wings are totally covered. Serve warm or chilled.

Serves 8

Mr. Spice sauces may be ordered at www.glutenfreemall.com.

Potato Skins with Cheese and Bacon

3   medium baking potatoes
1   tablespoon vegetable oil
5   slices Oscar Mayer bacon
4   ounces Cheddar cheese (such as
     Heluva® Good), shredded (1 cup)

4   ounces Monterey Jack cheese
     (such as Heluva® Good), shredded
     (1 cup)
1   tablespoon minced fresh chives

Preheat oven to 425°. Scrub potatoes and pat dry. Prick skins with fork on each side. Bake for 1 hour. Cool slightly. Cut each potato lengthwise into quarters. Scoop out pulp from centers, leaving ½-inch thick layer of cooked potato on skins. Reserve pulp for another use.

Place potato skins on baking sheet. Brush insides of skins with oil and season with salt and pepper. Cut bacon into 1-inch pieces and cook in a skillet over medium heat until brown and crisp. Drain on paper towels. Crumble into a medium bowl. Add cheeses and stir to blend. Sprinkle cheese evenly on top of skins. Bake until skins are crisp and cheese mixture melts, about 25 minutes. Transfer skins to serving platter; sprinkle with chives and top with a dollop of sour cream.

Serves 6

Cherry Tomatoes with Tuna

1   can (6-ounces) tuna in water (such   2   garlic cloves, minced
    as Bumble Bee), well drained   1   tablespoon fresh lemon juice
¼   cup plain nonfat yogurt   20 cherry tomatoes
¼   cup minced shallots

Using a serrated knife, slice about ⅛-inch from the top of each tomato. If the tomato
does not sit upright, trim a tiny slice from the bottom. Using a small knife or melon
baller, scoop out the seeds. Place tuna in a medium bowl. Flake with a fork. Mix in
yogurt, shallots, garlic, and lemon juice. Spoon tuna mixture into tomatoes.

Serves 10

Cucumber Cups with Tuna

1   English cucumber
1   can (6 ounces) tuna in water
      (such as Bumble Bee)

2   tablespoons mayonnaise
      (such as Hellmann's)
¼   cup finely chopped onion

Peel cucumbers and cut crosswise into ½-inch pieces. With a small melon baller, scoop out some of the seeds from the center of each piece, leaving ¼-inch at the bottom. Drain tuna and place in a medium bowl. Flake with a fork. Mix in mayonnaise and onion. Spoon tuna mixture into cucumber cups.

Serves 16

Cucumber cups may be prepared up to 4 hours in advance.
Cover and chill. Tuna mixture is best if prepared just before serving.

Hard-Cooked Eggs

12 large eggs

Place eggs in a large saucepan. Add enough water to cover eggs. Bring to a boil over high heat. Remove from heat and cover. Let stand for 25 minutes. Pour off water and fill pan with cold water. Let stand at least 2 minutes. To remove shells, gently tap egg on counter top and peel off the eggshell.

Serves 6

Deviled Eggs

6 large hard-cooked eggs, cooled and peeled
½ teaspoon salt
½ teaspoon McCormick ground mustard

Freshly ground black pepper
3 tablespoons Kraft Miracle Whip® or Hellmann's mayonnaise
McCormick paprika

Cut eggs in half lengthwise. Carefully remove yolks and mash with a fork. Add salt, mustard, pepper, and mayonnaise and mix well. Divide yolk mixture among egg halves, mounding slightly. Sprinkle with paprika.

Serves 12

Red Beet Eggs

1   can (14.5 ounces) sliced beets (such as Del Monte)

1   cup Heinz apple cider vinegar

½   cup sugar

1   teaspoon salt

5   whole cloves

1   McCormick cinnamon stick

6   large hard-cooked eggs, peeled

Drain and measure juice from beets. Add enough water to make 1 cup. In a medium nonaluminum saucepan, combine beet juice, vinegar, sugar, salt, cloves, and cinnamon stick. Bring to a boil over medium heat, stirring to dissolve sugar. Cool 10 minutes, remove cinnamon stick and pour hot liquid over beets in a quart size glass jar. Let stand 24 hours in refrigerator. Add hard-cooked eggs; let stand in juices 24 hours so that flavor penetrates the whole egg. Cut eggs in half and serve on a platter with the pickled beets.

Serves 12

This is a traditional Pennsylvania Dutch recipe passed down from my grandmother. The beet juice penetrates the egg white and turns it a lovely shade of magenta. Great for snacking and a must for every picnic! Please go to the Consumer FAQs at heinz.com to confirm the gluten-free status of Heinz Apple Cider Vinegar. Please note that Heinz Apple Cider Flavored Vinegar is not gluten-free.

Taco Dip

2 tablespoons Old El Paso® mild taco seasoning mix

1 can (16 ounces) Old El Paso® refried beans

2 avocados, mashed

1 cup Breakstone's sour cream

½ cup green onion, chopped

1 (4-ounce) can sliced black olives, drained

1 (4-ounce) can Ortega diced green chiles, drained

4 ounces Cheddar cheese (such as Heluva® Good), shredded (1 cup)

2 medium tomatoes, chopped

1 bag Tostitos chips

Stir taco seasoning into refried beans and mix well. Combine mashed avocados with sour cream and mix well. Layer ingredients on a serving platter in the following order: refried beans, sour cream, onions, olives, chiles, Cheddar cheese, and tomatoes. Circle the plate with Tostitos chips.

Serves 12

Hot Crab Dip with Toast Rounds

4 ounces Philadelphia cream cheese, softened

2 tablespoons Breakstone's sour cream

1 clove garlic, minced or pressed

2 tablespoons finely chopped onion

1 tablespoon Lea & Perrins Worcestershire sauce

1 teaspoon Maille Dijon style mustard

1 teaspoon prepared horseradish (such as Heluva® Good)

1 teaspoon lemon juice

2 (3.53 ounces) pouches Chicken of the Sea® Premium Crab

Freshly ground black pepper

1 tablespoon freshly grated Parmesan cheese (such as Stella)

Preheat oven to 350°. In a medium bowl, mix the cream cheese, sour cream, garlic, onion, Worcestershire sauce, mustard, horseradish, and lemon juice. Add the crabmeat and season with pepper. Transfer to an 8 x 11-inch baking dish. Sprinkle with Parmesan cheese. Bake until golden brown and bubbly, about 20 to 30 minutes.

Serves 12

Toast Rounds:

7 slices Kinnikinnick Italian White Tapioca Rice Bread

Preheat oven to 450°. Cut rounds from the bread with a 1⅓-inch round cookie cutter. Place the bread rounds on a baking sheet and bake for 5 to 6 minutes until golden brown. Let cool for a minute or 2, then remove from baking sheet and allow to cool on a rack.

Dip can be prepared several hours ahead and refrigerated until baking.
Serve with toast rounds or Green Mountain Gringo Tortilla Strips. Kinnikinnick
products may be ordered at www.goglutenfree.com or call (877) 503-4466.

Party Mix

¼ cup (½ stick) butter

2 tablespoons Lea & Perrins Worcestershire sauce

1¼ teaspoons Lawry's seasoned salt

¾ tablespoon McCormick garlic powder

½ tablespoon McCormick onion powder

4 cups Health Valley Rice Crunch-Ems cereal

2 cups EnviroKidz Gorilla Munch cereal

1½ cups Planter's mixed nuts

1 cup Glutano pretzels

Preheat oven to 250°. Melt butter in microwave on High (100 percent power) for 30 seconds. Stir in Worcestershire sauce, salt, garlic powder, and onion powder. In a large mixing bowl, combine Rice Crunch-Ems cereal, Gorilla Munch cereal, mixed nuts, and pretzels. Gradually stir in melted butter mixture until evenly coated. Transfer cereal mixture to a 15 x 10 x 1-inch baking pan and spread evenly. Bake 1 hour, stirring every 15 minutes. Spread on paper towels to cool. Store in a large Ziploc bag.

Serves 12

Please call Unilever Consumer Services (800) 952-9797
to confirm gluten-free status of Lawry's Seasoned Salt.

Trail Mix

¾ cup peanuts (such as Planter's dry roasted)

⅓ cup M&Ms® plain chocolate candies

1 (1½-ounce) package raisins (⅓ cup)

2 tablespoons almonds (such as Blue Diamond Whole Natural Almonds)

Combine peanuts, chocolate candies, raisins, and almonds in a small bowl. Store in an airtight container.

Serves 2

A perfect snack for hiking, skiing, or anytime you need an energy boost.

Peanut Butter Waffle Snacks

1   Van's wheat-free mini waffle   ½   banana, sliced
1   tablespoon peanut butter
    (such as Simply Jif)

Toast waffle and cool slightly. Divide into 4 mini-waffles. Spread each mini-waffle with peanut butter and top with 1 or 2 banana slices.

Serves 1

To avoid cross contamination, a separate toaster should
be used for gluten-free foods. A toaster oven, where the rack can be removed
and washed if others have used it may be a good alternative.

Popcorn Balls

1   cup sugar
⅓   cup water
⅓   cup Karo light corn syrup
1   teaspoon salt

¼   cup butter
7   cups popped microwave popcorn
     (Such as Orville Redenbacher's
     Butter)

Combine sugar, butter, and corn syrup in heavy medium saucepan. Whisk over medium-low heat until sugar dissolves and butter melts. Attach clip-on candy thermometer to side of pan. Increase heat to high and boil (without stirring) until thermometer registers 250°, about 4 minutes. Remove from heat. Stir in salt. Gradually pour syrup in a thin stream over popcorn, gently stirring to coat popcorn completely. Shape, with buttered hands, into balls.

Serves 12

Cranberry-Orange Juice

4   ounces orange juice (such as   4   ounces Ocean Spray cranberry juice
    Tropicana Pure Premium)   cocktail

Pour orange juice into a 10-ounce glass. Add cranberry juice cocktail. Serve.

Serves 1

Raspberry Lemonade

1   package (10-ounce) Cascadian
    Farm® frozen organic raspberries
1¼ cups fresh lemon juice
    (about 8 lemons)

1   cup sugar
3   cups water

Heat water in 4-cup glass measuring cup in microwave on high for 2 minutes. Mix in sugar, stirring until dissolved. Cool to room temperature. In a blender, purée berries with 1 cup cooled sugar syrup and lemon juice. Pour purée through a sieve into a 2-quart pitcher. Mix in remaining sugar syrup and stir. Fill pitcher with ice. Fill 4 glasses with ice and add lemonade.

Serves 4

Strawberry Margaritas

16 ounces fresh strawberries
2½ cups crushed ice
½   cup fresh lime juice (from 2 limes)

¼   cup sugar
6   ounces Sprite
    Lime wedges (optional)

Combine ice, lime juice, strawberries, sugar, and Sprite in a blender and process until smooth. Pour the margaritas into 4 large glasses. Garnish margaritas with a lime wedge, if desired. Serve immediately.

Serves 4

Strawberry-Mint Lemonade

¾ cup water
1¾ cups sugar
2¼ cups sliced strawberries (about 1 pint)
2 tablespoons fresh mint leaves

1½ cups fresh lemon juice
   (from 9 lemons)
24 ounces chilled sparkling mineral
   water (such as Perrier)
   Fresh mint leaves, for garnish

In a heavy saucepan, bring water and sugar to a simmer over medium-high heat. Simmer for 2 to 3 minutes, stirring to dissolve the sugar completely. Remove from the heat and cool syrup to room temperature. In a blender, purée berries with syrup, mint, and lemon juice. Pour purée through a sieve into a 2 quart pitcher. You may need to rinse sieve several times to clear the strawberry seeds. Stir in sparkling water. Serve sparkling lemonade over ice, garnished with fresh mint leaves.

Serves 10

To confirm the gluten-free status of
Perrier Sparkling Natural Mineral Water, please call (800) 937-2002.

Raspberry Mango Smoothie

1 whole frozen banana, sliced
1 cup orange juice or orange Gatorade
1 cup chopped mango

½ cup Cascadian Farm® frozen organic raspberries

Combine the mango and orange juice (or Gatorade) in a blender; process until smooth. Add the banana and raspberries. Blend until smooth. Serve immediately.

Serves 2

Smoothies make an ideal after-school snack.

Piña Colada Smoothie

1   cup Pineapple Snapple-A-Day Meal   3   scoops Edy's Grand vanilla ice
     Replacement   cream (or Dreyer's)

Combine Snapple-A-Day and ice cream in a blender or milk shake maker. Blend until smooth, about 2 minutes.

Serves 1

Lemon and Raspberry Smoothie

½ cup Cascadian Farm® frozen organic raspberries

½ cup Hagen-Dazs® zesty lemon sorbet

1 cup orange juice (such as Tropicana Pure Premium)

¼ cup crushed ice

Combine all ingredients in a blender (ice last). Blend until smooth.

Serves 2

Strawberry-Peach Smoothie

1	medium banana, sliced	¾	cup peaches, sliced and peeled
1	cup orange juice (such as Tropicana Pure Premium)	¾	cup sliced strawberries

Combine all ingredients in a blender; process until smooth. Serve immediately.

Serves 3

Yogurt Smoothie

6   ounces Yoplait® original red
    raspberry yogurt
½   cup skim milk
1   cup Cascadian Farm® frozen organic
    raspberries

1   frozen banana, sliced
½   cup orange juice (such as Tropicana
    Pure Premium)

Combine the milk and yogurt in a blender. Add the raspberries, banana, and orange juice. Blend until smooth. Serve immediately.

Serves 2

Chocolate Milk Shake

1   scoop Edy's Grand vanilla ice cream (or Dreyer's)

1   scoop Edy's Grand chocolate ice cream (or Dreyer's)

½   cup whole milk

Place ingredients in blender or milk shake maker. Blend until smooth, about 2 minutes.

Serves 1

Chocolate Strawberry Shake

½ cup whole milk

2 large scoops Edy's Grand Chocolate Ice Cream (or Dreyer's)

1 cup Cascadian Farm® frozen organic strawberries

Place milk, ice cream, and strawberries in blender. Cover and blend until smooth, about 2 minutes.

Serves 1

Orange Frosty Shake

3 scoops Edy's Grand vanilla ice cream (or Dreyer's)

1½ cups orange juice (such as Tropicana Pure Premium)

Combine ice cream and orange juice in a blender or milkshake maker. Blend until smooth, about 2 minutes.

Serves 2

BRUNCHES & BREADS

Brunches & Breads

Andrew's Breakfast

1 cup chopped breakfast ham (such as Dietz and Watson or Hormel® Cure 81®)

½ medium sweet onion, chopped

1 medium baking potato, baked and cut into ¼-inch slices

3 large eggs

1 tablespoon butter

Salt and freshly ground black pepper

In a large nonstick skillet, cook onion and potatoes in butter over medium heat until onions are tender and potatoes are lightly browned, about 10 minutes. Add ham, and reduce heat to medium-low. Season with salt and pepper. Clear a spot in the middle of the pan and add the eggs. Fry eggs until bottoms are white then flip to cook tops. Mix eggs up slightly with potato and ham mixture. Continue cooking over low heat until eggs are cooked. Serve immediately.

Serves 2

When making baked potatoes for dinner,
always bake a few extras to have leftover with breakfast.

Asparagus Frittata

1 pound asparagus, cut into ½-inch
   lengths

5 extra large eggs

⅔ cup freshly grated Parmesan cheese
   (such as Stella)

¼ teaspoon salt
   Freshly ground black pepper

3 tablespoons butter

Cook asparagus in a large saucepan of boiling water until crisp-tender, about 4 minutes. Allow asparagus to cool. Beat the eggs in a bowl until the yolks and whites are blended. Add the asparagus, salt, pepper, and grated cheese and mix thoroughly. In a large ovenproof skillet, melt the butter over medium heat. When it begins to foam, add the egg mixture, turn down the heat as low as possible. When the eggs have set and thickened and only the top surface is runny, about 15 minutes of very slow cooking, run the skillet under the broiler until the top face of the frittata has set, about 30 seconds. The frittata should be set, but soft. It should not be browned either on the bottom or top side. Loosen the frittata with a spatula and slide it onto a serving platter. Cut into 4 wedges and serve.

Serves 4

California Eggs

6 large eggs, slightly beaten
1 cup whole milk
16 ounces Heluva® Good Monterey Jack cheese, shredded (4 cups)
¾ cup Really Great Food Company biscuit mix
16 ounces small curd cottage cheese (such as Breakstone's)
1⅓ cups chopped breakfast ham (such as Dietz and Watson or Cure 81®)
5 green onions, sliced
1 teaspoon butter, to grease pan

Preheat oven to 350°. Grease a 9 x 13 baking dish with butter. In a large mixing bowl, beat eggs lightly with milk and add cheese, biscuit mix, cottage cheese, ham, and green onions. Pour egg mixture into baking dish and bake, uncovered, for 40 to 45 minutes until set and lightly browned. Let stand 5 minutes before cutting into squares.

Serves 12

Please go to the FAQs at www.dietzandwatson.com or Hormel.com
to determine the gluten-free status of Dietz and Watson ham.

Eggs McAndrew

2 slices Kinnikinnick Italian White Tapioca Rice Bread, toasted

2 slices breakfast ham (such as Dietz and Watson or Cure 81®)

2 slices cheese (such as Kraft Singles)

2 eggs, poached or fried

Place toast on aluminum foil and top with cheese. Toast in toaster oven until cheese melts. Meanwhile, cook ham in a small nonstick sauté pan over medium heat until browned, turning once, about 4 minutes. Place toast and cheese on individual plates. Top with ham slice and egg. Serve immediately.

Serves 2

Please go to the FAQs at www.dietzandwatson.com or Hormel.com to determine the gluten-free status of Dietz and Watson ham. Kinnikinnick products can be ordered at www.goglutenfree.com or call (877) 503-4466.

Ham and Onion Quiche

3 cups Cascadian Farm® organic hash browns

¼ cup butter, melted

⅔ cup chopped breakfast ham (such as Dietz and Watson or Hormel Cure 81®)

5 large eggs

¼ cup finely chopped onion

2 ounces Cheddar cheese (such as Heluva® Good), shredded (½ cup)

1 ounce Monterey Jack cheese (such as Heluva® Good), shredded (¼ cup)

Salt and freshly ground black pepper

¾ cup whole milk

Preheat oven to 425°. Butter a 9-inch pie plate. In a shallow baking dish, defrost potatoes in microwave for 3 to 4 minutes, or until any large chunks of potato can be crumbled apart. Add melted butter to potatoes and press into bottom and sides of pie plate. Bake for 30 minutes. Reduce oven temperature to 350°. In a large mixing bowl, whisk eggs and milk. Add the onion, cheese, ham, salt, and pepper. Pour egg mixture into crust. Bake quiche for 40 minutes, or until a knife inserted into the center comes out clean. Cool for 5 minutes. Cut quiche into wedges and serve.

Serves 4

I like to use my Emile Henry pie plate for this recipe.

Mini Ham and Cheese Frittatas

1 tablespoon extra light olive oil
½ cup finely chopped onion
⅔ cup chopped breakfast ham (such as Dietz and Watson or Hormel Cure 81®)
2 ounces Cheddar cheese (such as Heluva® Good), shredded (½ cup)

2 tablespoons chopped fresh chives
⅛ teaspoon McCormick thyme leaves
3 egg whites, whisked
2 large eggs, whisked
Freshly ground black pepper

Preheat oven to 350°. Butter 24 miniature muffin cups. Heat 1 tablespoon oil in a large nonstick skillet over medium heat. Add onion and cook and stir until softened, about 4 minutes. Add ham and cook and stir 3 minutes. Remove from heat and cool. In a large bowl, combine cheese, chives, thyme, egg whites, and eggs. Season with pepper. Stir to combine. Add ham mixture and stir to combine. Spoon mixture into miniature muffin cups and bake at 350° for 18 minutes or until set. Frittatas may be served hot or at room temperature.

Serves 8

Please go to the FAQs at www.dietzandwatson.com
or www.hormel.com to review gluten-free status of ham.

Rocky Mountain Eggs

2 tablespoons butter, to grease pan
12 ounces Jimmy Dean regular flavor
   fresh premium pork sausage
1 medium baking potato, baked,
   peeled and sliced ¼-inch thick
1 medium onion, chopped

10 large eggs
¼ cup whole milk
4 ounces Cheddar cheese (such as
   Heluva® Good), shredded (1 cup)
½ pound Oscar Mayer bacon, cooked
   and crumbled

Heat oven to 350° (325°F if using a glass baking dish). Grease an 8 x 8 or 9 x 13-inch baking dish. In a large skillet, cook sausage over medium-high heat, stirring frequently until thoroughly cooked and no longer pink. Spread sausage in the pan. Arrange potatoes over the sausage and spread onions over the top. Whisk eggs and milk. Pour egg mixture slowly over the sausage and potatoes. Scatter the shredded cheese over the top and sprinkle with bacon. Bake uncovered until knife inserted comes out clean, about 45 minutes. Let stand 5 to 10 minutes before cutting.

Serves 6

My husband and son brought this recipe home from a Boy Scout ski trip.

Sausage Scrambled Eggs

6 ounces Jimmy Dean regular flavor
    premium pork sausage

2 tablespoons vegetable oil
10 large eggs

In a large nonstick skillet, heat the olive oil over medium heat. Add the sausage and cook, stirring and breaking up meat until browned, 4 to 5 minutes. Whisk eggs together in a bowl and stir into sausage. Cook, stirring, until eggs are scrambled and just set, about 5 minutes. Serve immediately.

Serves 4

Steak and Eggs

6	slices cooked steak	4	large eggs
1	baking potato, baked, peeled, and sliced ¼-inch thick	2	tablespoons butter
½	cup chopped onion	1	tablespoon vegetable oil
			Salt and freshly ground black pepper

Heat 1 tablespoon butter and 1 tablespoon oil in a large nonstick skillet over medium heat. Add onion; cook and stir 4 minutes. Add potato and cook, turning occasionally for 10 minutes until lightly browned. Add the remaining 1 tablespoon butter if needed to prevent sticking. Season with salt and pepper. Move potatoes to the side and add steak slices. Warm steak for about 1 minute, turning to heat on both sides. While potatoes are cooking, heat 1 tablespoon oil in a medium nonstick skillet over medium-low heat. Break the eggs into the pan, reduce heat to low, and cook until the whites are set and the yolks are done as desired. Turn eggs over and cook tops for 30 seconds. Transfer the steak, potatoes, and eggs to individual plates and serve.

Serves 2

Potatoes may be baked ahead of time and stored for up to 2 days in the refrigerator.

Home Fries

2	baking potatoes, baked and chilled	½ cup chopped onion
3	tablespoons butter	Salt and freshly ground black pepper
1	tablespoon vegetable oil	

Cut potatoes crosswise into ¼-inch slices. Heat butter and oil in a large nonstick skillet over moderately low heat. Add onions and cook, stirring occasionally, about 4 minutes. Add potatoes and cook, turning occasionally, until lightly browned, about 10 minutes. Season with salt and pepper.

Serves 2

Potatoes may be baked ahead of time and stored for up to 2 days in the refrigerator.

Banana Pancakes

1   cup Mona's pancake/waffle mix
1   large egg
1   cup buttermilk
2   tablespoons vegetable oil

1   large ripe banana, sliced thin
½   cup pure maple syrup (or Aunt
    Jemima® Lite syrup)

In a medium bowl, add pancake mix, egg, milk and oil. Whisk until combined. Lightly grease a griddle or heavy skillet and heat over medium heat. Pour batter onto the griddle using a ¼ cup measure. When the tops of the pancakes begin to bubble, cover them with 6-8 banana slices. When the pancakes are golden brown on the bottom, flip them over and continue to cook until the second side is golden brown, about 2 minutes longer. Heat maple syrup in microwave for 30 seconds on High. Serve pancakes warm with syrup.

2 servings

Pancake mix made be ordered at www.madebymona.com
or call (866) 486-0701 toll free.

Buttermilk Pancakes

1 cup Mona's pancake/waffle mix
1 large egg
1 cup buttermilk

2 tablespoons vegetable oil
½ cup pure maple syrup (or Aunt Jemima® Lite syrup)

In a medium bowl, add pancake mix, egg, buttermilk, and oil. Whisk until combined. Lightly grease a griddle or heavy skillet and heat over medium heat. Pour batter onto the griddle using a ¼ cup measure. When the tops of the pancakes bubble and the edges start to dry, flip them over and continue to cook until the second side is golden brown, about 2 minutes. Heat syrup in microwave for 30 seconds on High. Serve pancakes warm with syrup.

Serves 2

Pancake mix may be ordered at www.madebymona.com
or call (866) 486-0701 toll free.

Apple Cinnamon Waffles

1   (24-ounce) package Pamela's
      pancake & baking mix (5¼ cups)
2⅔ cups water

½   cup vegetable oil
8   large eggs, separated
2   medium apples, chopped

   Whip egg whites with a large balloon whisk until frothy. In a separate bowl, combine
Pamela's mix, egg yolks, water, and oil. Mix until smooth. Add cinnamon and chopped
apple. Fold in egg whites. Pour batter using a ½ cup measuring cup onto a pre-heated
waffle iron sprayed lightly with PAM cooking spray. (For additional batches, there is no
need to spray with additional cooking spray.) Bake until golden brown. Serve
immediately or freeze and reheat in toaster.

Serves 12

To make waffles I use my VillaWare® Classic Waffler
with the setting on medium-high (5½). It bakes four 4½-inch waffles.

Blueberry Waffles

2⅔ cups Pamela's pancake & baking
    mix

1⅓ cups water

¼ cup vegetable oil

4 large eggs, separated

1 cup fresh blueberries (or Cascadian
    Farm® frozen organic blueberries)

Whip egg whites until frothy. In a separate bowl, combine Pamela's mix, egg yolks, water, and oil. Mix until there are no lumps. Fold in egg whites and blueberries. Pour with ½ cup measuring cup onto a pre-heated waffle iron sprayed lightly with PAM cooking spray. Bake until golden brown. Serve immediately or freeze and reheat in toaster.

Serves 6

Pumpkin Walnut Waffles

2⅔ cups Pamela's pancake & baking mix

1⅓ cups water

¼ cup vegetable oil

4 large eggs, separated

¾ cup Libby's 100% pure pumpkin

1 tablespoon McCormick cinnamon

¼ teaspoon McCormick ground cloves

¼ teaspoon McCormick ground ginger

¾ teaspoon McCormick pure vanilla extract

½ cup walnuts, finely chopped

Whisk egg whites with a large balloon whisk until frothy. In a separate bowl, combine Pamela's mix, egg yolks, water, and oil. Mix until smooth. Add pumpkin, spices, and walnuts. Fold in egg whites. Pour batter using a ½ cup measuring cup onto a pre-heated waffle iron sprayed lightly with PAM cooking spray. (For additional batches, there is no need to spray with additional cooking spray.) Bake until golden brown. Serve immediately or freeze and reheat in toaster.

Serves 6

French Toast

8 slices Mr. Ritt's challah bread	¼ cup milk
6 large eggs	1 cup pure maple syrup
1 teaspoon McCormick pure vanilla	(or Aunt Jemima® Lite syrup)
extract	½ teaspoon McCormick cinnamon

Lightly oil a nonstick skillet or griddle. Whisk eggs, milk, vanilla extract, and cinnamon in a shallow bowl. Dip bread slices into egg mixture and cook over medium heat until browned. Flip over and cook until second side is browned. Heat syrup in microwave for 30 seconds on High. Serve French toast warm with syrup.

Serves 4

Challah bread can be ordered from
Mr. Ritt's bakery in Philadelphia. Call (215) 627-3034.

Anne's Apple Upside-Down Cake

For Topping:

3 tablespoons unsalted butter
½ cup firmly packed Domino® light brown sugar

2 large Granny Smith apples, peeled, cored and cut into thin slices

Preheat oven to 375°. To make topping, heat butter in a saucepan over moderate heat. Stir in brown sugar and remove from heat. Spread mixture evenly in pie plate and arrange apples, overlapping, in one layer.

For Cake:

1 cup Really Great Food Company biscuit mix
¼ cup sugar
½ teaspoon McCormick cinnamon

5 tablespoons cold unsalted butter, cut into pieces
½ cup buttermilk

To make cake, blend biscuit mix, sugar, and cinnamon in a food processor. Add butter and pulse until mixture resembles coarse meal. Transfer to a bowl and add buttermilk, stirring just until mixture is moistened. Drop batter on top of apples and gently spread, leaving a 1-inch border around edge of pie plate. Bake cake in middle of oven until golden brown and firm to the touch, 25 to 30 minutes. Cool cake in pie plate on a rack 3 minutes, then invert onto a platter. Serve warm.

Serves 8

Really Great Food Company products may be ordered
at www.reallygreatfood.com or call (800) 593-5377.

Blueberry Corn Muffins

½   cup Bob's Red Mill rice flour
¼   cup Bob's Red Mill potato starch
¼   cup Bob's Red Mill tapioca flour
¾   cup Kinnikinnick cornmeal
¼   cup sugar
2   teaspoons Rumford baking powder
½   teaspoon salt

1½ cups fresh blueberries (or frozen blueberries such as Cascadian Farms, thawed)
1   large egg
½   cup buttermilk
½   cup (1 stick) butter, melted

Preheat oven to 425°. Grease muffin tins. Mix dry ingredients in a large bowl. Stir in blueberries. Beat egg, buttermilk, and melted butter in medium bowl. Add to flour mixture and stir just until flour is moistened. Spoon into muffin tins, filling two-thirds full. Bake until golden, 20 to 25 minutes. Serve warm.

Serves 12

Bob's Red Mill flour can be ordered
at www.bobsredmill.com or call (800) 349-2173.
Kinnikinnick products can be ordered
at www.goglutenfree.com or call (877) 503-4466.

Banana Mini-Muffins

2 cups Mona's Multi Mix
1 teaspoon Calumet baking soda
¾ teaspoon Rumford baking powder
½ cup sugar
½ cup Domino® light brown sugar

2 large eggs
2 tablespoons Breakstone's sour cream
1½ cups ripe banana (3 large bananas), mashed

Preheat oven to 325° and use paper mini-muffin cups to fill mini-muffin tin. Combine Mona's Multi Mix, baking soda, and baking powder in a small bowl; whisk to combine and set aside. In a large bowl, beat eggs and sugars until blended. Add sour cream and mashed banana. Gradually beat in flour mix and stir until batter is thoroughly blended. Fill mini-muffin cups about ½ full using a cookie scoop. Bake 15 minutes or until a toothpick comes out clean. Let muffins cool in pan for 5 minutes, then remove to rack to cool completely.

Serves 12

Using a cookie scoop ensures that muffins will be uniform in size.
Cookie scoops are available at kitchen and houseware stores. Multi Mix may
be ordered at www.madebymona.com or call (866) 486-0701 toll free.

Mark's Banana Bread

1 cup Bob's Red Mill garbanzo & fava flour

½ cup Bob's Red Mill brown rice flour

½ cup Bob's Red Mill tapioca flour

1 teaspoon Calumet baking soda

1 teaspoon Rumford baking powder

½ cup Crisco vegetable shortening

1 cup sugar

2 large eggs, whisked

2 tablespoons Breakstone's sour cream

1½ cups mashed ripe bananas (about 3 large)

Preheat the oven to 300°. Lightly grease four small loaf pans (4½ x 2¾-inch) with Crisco shortening. Combine flour, baking soda, and baking powder in a small bowl; mix with whisk. In a large mixing bowl, beat the shortening and sugar until blended. Add whisked eggs, sour cream, and mashed banana. Gradually beat in flour mixture and stir just until the batter is thoroughly blended.

Pour batter into prepared pans and bake for about 25 to 30 minutes, or until a toothpick inserted into the center of the bread comes out clean. Bread will be flat on top. Remove from the oven, and let cool in the pan for 5 minutes, then turn out onto a rack to cool completely.

Serves 12

Bob's Red Mill flour can be ordered
at www.bobsredmill.com or call (800) 349-2173.

Raspberry Cream Cheese Coffee Cake

Cake:

2½ cups Mona's Multi Mix
¾ cup sugar
¾ cup (1½ sticks) butter
½ teaspoon Rumford baking powder
½ teaspoon Calumet baking soda

¼ teaspoon salt
¾ cup Breakstone's sour cream
1 large egg, lightly beaten
2 teaspoons McCormick pure vanilla extract

Preheat oven to 350°. Grease and flour a 9-inch springform pan. In a large bowl, combine flour and sugar; cut in the butter, using a pastry blender or two knives, until the mixture resembles coarse crumbs. Remove 1 cup for topping. Add baking powder, baking soda, salt, sour cream, egg, and vanilla to remaining crumb mixture. Blend well. Spread dough over bottom and 2 inches up the sides of the prepared springform pan. Dough should be ¼-inch thick on all sides.

Filling:

8 ounces Philadelphia cream cheese
¼ cup sugar

1 large egg
⅔ cup Stonewall Kitchen Raspberry Peach Champagne jam

In a small bowl, combine cream cheese, sugar, and egg; blend well. Pour over dough in springform pan. Carefully spoon jam evenly over cheese mixture.

Topping:

½ cup sliced almonds (optional)

In a small bowl, combine reserved crumb mixture and the almonds. Sprinkle over the top. Bake for 50 to 60 minutes, or until cream cheese filling is set and the crust is a deep golden brown. Cool in the pan for 15 minutes. Remove the sides of the pan. Serve warm or cool. Cover and refrigerate leftovers.

Serves 8

This recipe is a gluten free adaptation of a recipe from stonewallkitchen.com.
The original recipe is from the Junior League Centennial Cookbook.

Sour Cream Coffee Cake

Topping:

2   tablespoons butter, softened
¼   cup sugar

½   teaspoon McCormick cinnamon

Preheat oven to 350°. Grease a 9-inch round cake pan. To make the topping, mix the butter, sugar, and cinnamon together in a small bowl using a pastry blender. Set aside.

Cake:

1   large egg
¼   cup sour cream (such as Breakstone's)
⅔   cup milk

1   teaspoon McCormick pure vanilla extract
2   cups Mona's Happy Day cake mix

Combine the eggs and sour cream in a large mixing bowl and beat until well blended. Add milk and vanilla and beat until combined. Add the cake mix and beat until smooth. Spread the cake batter in the prepared pan and sprinkle with the topping mixture. Cut in topping, holding knife point-down, and make a swirl pattern through the batter. Bake approximately 35 minutes, or until a toothpick inserted in the middle come out clean. Set on a rack to cool for 5 minutes; run a knife around edges of the pan, and turn the cake out onto a rack. Let sit to cool slightly, about 10 minutes. Serve warm.

Serves 8

Cake mix may be ordered at www.madebymona.com
or call (866) 486-0701 toll free.

Soups, Salads & Sandwiches

Soups, Salads & Sandwiches

Broccoli and Cheddar Chowder

1 pound broccoli (about 2 cups florets)

2 tablespoons extra light olive oil

1 large onion, chopped

1 red bell pepper, chopped

1 large garlic clove, finely chopped or pressed

1 teaspoon McCormick ground cumin

1 teaspoon salt

½ teaspoon McCormick ground mustard

Freshly ground black pepper

1½ tablespoons potato flour (such as Bob's Red Mill)

8 ounces Kitchen Basics chicken stock

1 large baking potato, baked, peeled and cut into ½-inch cubes

6 ounces Cheddar cheese (such as Heluva® Good), shredded (1½ cups)

¾ cup half-and-half

Trim broccoli stems from florets and chop into ¼-inch pieces. Cut remaining broccoli into small florets. Cook florets in a large pot of boiling salted water until just tender, about 2 minutes. Reserve 2 cups cooking water for chowder. Drain.

In a medium saucepan, heat the oil over medium heat. Add onion, bell pepper, broccoli stems, and garlic. Cook and stir until onion is softened, about 8 minutes. Add cumin, salt, and mustard. Season with pepper. Cook, stirring constantly, 1 minute. Add potato flour and cook, stirring constantly, 2 minutes. Add reserved cooking water, chicken stock, and potato. Simmer (partially covered), stirring occasionally, about 10 minutes.

Purée about 2 cups of chowder in a blender until smooth (use caution when blending hot liquids) and return to pot. Stir in cheese and half-and-half. Cook and stir until cheese is melted. Add florets and cook over medium heat, stirring occasionally, until heated through, about 2 minutes.

Serves 4

Potatoes may be baked ahead of time and stored for up to 2 days in the refrigerator. Bob's Red Mill flour can be ordered at www.bobsredmill.com or call (800) 349-2173.

Caesar Salad

¼ cup Kraft Miracle Whip® or Hellmann's® or Best Foods® Real Mayonnaise

1 tablespoon red wine vinegar (such as Regina)

1½ tablespoons fresh lemon juice

1 teaspoon McCormick ground mustard

½ cup extra virgin olive oil

1 teaspoon Worcestershire sauce

2 cloves garlic, minced or pressed

⅛ teaspoon sea salt

1 package (10 ounces) Hearts of Romaine lettuce

⅓ cup freshly grated Parmesan cheese (such as Frigo)

Freshly ground pepper

Combine mayonnaise, vinegar, lemon juice, mustard, oil, Worcestershire sauce, garlic, and salt in blender; purée until smooth. Place lettuce in large bowl. Toss with enough dressing to coat. Add Parmesan cheese and toss well. Season salad with freshly ground pepper. Serve with any remaining dressing.

Serves 6

Call (888) 887-3266 to confirm gluten-free status of Regina red wine vinegar.

Mandarin Orange Salad

10 ounces ready-to-eat romaine lettuce hearts (bite-size pieces)
½ small red onion, chopped
1 can (11-ounces) Dole Mandarin oranges in light syrup, drained
¼ cup slivered almonds

4 tablespoons Stonewall Kitchen balsamic vinegar
2 tablespoons sugar
⅓ cup extra virgin olive oil
1 teaspoon salt
1 envelope Good Seasons Italian Salad Dressing & Recipe Mix

Cook sliced almonds and sugar in a small nonstick skillet over medium-low heat, stirring constantly, 5 or 6 minutes or until sugar is dissolved and almonds are evenly coated. Remove from heat and set aside. Whisk together vinegar, oil, salt, and dressing mix. In a salad bowl, toss lettuce and onion. Drizzle with dressing and toss. Add almonds and oranges and toss.

Serves 6

Raspberry Spinach Salad

½ cup Regina raspberry balsamic
    vinegar
½ cup vegetable oil
½ cup sugar
1 teaspoon McCormick ground
    mustard

1 teaspoon poppy seeds
8 cups fresh baby spinach, rinsed
1 cup fresh raspberries
1 cup toasted pecans

Combine raspberry vinegar, oil, sugar, and mustard in blender for 5 minutes. Add poppy seeds to blended ingredients. Place the spinach in a large salad bowl. Pour the prepared dressing over the spinach and toss to coat. Top with raspberries and toasted pecans.

Serves 8

Toasting nuts brings out their flavor. To toast pecans, spread
nuts in a single layer in a shallow baking pan. Toast in a 350° oven
until golden brown, 3 to 5 minutes. Call (888) 887-3266 to confirm
gluten-free status of Regina red wine vinegar.

Balsamic Vinaigrette

3   tablespoons Stonewall Kitchen
    balsamic vinegar
2   tablespoons extra virgin olive oil

3   tablespoons vegetable oil
1   package Good Seasons Italian salad
    dressing mix

Combine all ingredients in a jar; cover tightly, and shake vigorously.

Serves 4

Please go to www.stonewallkitchen.com to
confirm gluten-free status of vinegar. Stonewall Kitchen products may
be ordered at www.stonewallkitchen.com or call (800) 207-5267.

Cobb Salad

Dressing:

3 tablespoons Regina red wine vinegar

1 tablespoon fresh lemon juice

2 teaspoons Maille Dijon style
   mustard

1 clove garlic, minced or pressed

½ teaspoon salt

½ cup extra virgin olive oil
   Freshly ground black pepper

Whisk vinegar, lemon juice, mustard, garlic, and salt in a medium bowl to blend. Gradually whisk in oil until mixture thickens slightly. Season with pepper.

Salad:

   Boneless chicken breast halves
   (1½ pounds total)

2 medium avocados

10 ounces ready-to-eat romaine lettuce
   hearts (bite-size pieces)

6 slices bacon, cooked until crisp and
   drained

3 medium plum tomatoes, seeded and
   cut into ½-inch pieces

3 ounces Boar's Head blue cheese

2 hard-cooked eggs, finely chopped

¼ cup finely chopped fresh chives

Bring 5 cups water to a boil in a Dutch oven. Add chicken and more water if needed to cover chicken. Reduce heat and cover. Simmer over low heat until chicken is tender, about 15 to 20 minutes. Cool 5 minutes; remove skin and cut into ½-inch cubes. Quarter avocados lengthwise, then pit and peel. Cut lengthwise into ¼-inch-thick slices. In a large glass salad bowl, add lettuce and spread with an even layer of chicken. Crumble bacon over chicken layer, then layer with tomatoes, cheese, avocados, eggs, and chives. Just before serving, drizzle with salad dressing and toss.

Serves 6

Please call the Boar's Head Nutrition Line at (800) 352-6277
to confirm the gluten-free status of the blue cheese.

Salad Niçoise

Vinaigrette:

2 teaspoons McCormick basil leaves
1 tablespoon extra virgin olive oil
1 tablespoon fresh lemon juice
1 tablespoon Regina red wine vinegar

1 teaspoon Maille Dijon style mustard
3 garlic cloves, halved
Freshly ground black pepper

To make vinaigrette, combine all ingredients in a blender; process until smooth.

Salad:

1 can (12 ounces) Bumble Bee Tuna, drained and separated into chunks
Freshly ground black pepper
10 small red potatoes (1 pound)
½ pound green beans, trimmed
4 cups torn romaine lettuce
3 medium tomatoes, each cut into 6 wedges

3 hard-cooked large eggs, quartered lengthwise
1 small yellow bell pepper, cut into strips
½ cup black olives
1 tablespoon fresh lemon juice

Drizzle lemon juice over tuna; season with pepper. Marinate in refrigerator 15 minutes. Steam potatoes, covered, 3 minutes. Add green beans, and steam, covered, an additional 8 minutes or until vegetables are crisp-tender; cool. Arrange lettuce on a large serving platter. Arrange tuna, potatoes, green beans, tomatoes, eggs, and bell pepper over lettuce. Top with olives. Drizzle vinaigrette over salad.

Serves 6

Please go to the Consumer FAQs at bumblebee.com to
confirm the gluten-free status of Bumble Bee canned seafood products.

Garden Tuna Salad

1 teaspoon lemon juice

1 can (6 ounces) Chicken of the Sea® solid white albacore tuna in spring water, drained and flaked

1 tablespoon mayonnaise (such as Hellmann's)

6 leaves romaine lettuce, torn

1 large tomato, chopped

½ medium cucumber, sliced

3 green onions, chopped

6 pitted black olives

In a medium bowl, drizzle lemon juice over tuna. Add mayonnaise, mixing lightly with a fork. In a large bowl, toss lettuce, tomato, cucumber, and green onions. Serve salad in salad bowls and top with tuna mixture and black olives.

Serves 2

Please go to the Consumer FAQs at chickenofthesea.com
to confirm the gluten-free status of Chicken of the Sea products.

Tuna Pasta Salad

3 tablespoons Kraft Miracle Whip® or Hellmann's® or Best Foods® Real Mayonnaise

1 tablespoon fresh lemon juice

2 cups Tinkyada pasta shells, prepared as directed on package

1 can (6 ounces) Chicken of the Sea solid white tuna, drained and flaked

½ cup Green Giant frozen peas, defrosted

Lettuce, for serving

In a large bowl, combine tuna and lemon juice. Add mayonnaise and stir to combine. Add pasta. Gently stir in peas. Cover and chill 30 minutes. Serve over lettuce.

Serves 4

Please go to the Consumer FAQs at chickenofthesea.com to confirm the gluten-free status of Chicken of the Sea products.

Waldorf Chicken Salad

2   cups cooked chicken, cubed
1   cup chopped apples
¾   cup grapes, halved
½   cup thinly sliced celery
½   cup raisins

¼   cup walnuts, chopped
¼   cup Kraft Miracle Whip® or
      Hellmann's® or Best Foods® Real
      Mayonnaise
2   tablespoons fresh lemon juice
      Lettuce leaves, if desired

In a salad bowl, combine chicken, apples, grapes, celery, raisins, and walnuts. In a small bowl, whisk mayonnaise and lemon juice. Add to salad and toss gently to coat. Serve on lettuce.

Serves 4

Black Bean and Rice Salad

1 cup long-grain rice (Carolina or Mahatma), cooked

1 can (15 ounces) Progresso black beans, drained and rinsed

1 red bell pepper, chopped

1 yellow bell pepper, chopped

1 small red onion, cut into thin slices, then chopped

¼ cup fresh cilantro leaves

¼ cup extra light olive oil

3 tablespoons lime juice, from 2 limes

3 tablespoons Regina red wine vinegar

1 teaspoon McCormick ground cumin

1 teaspoon McCormick chili powder

Whisk oil, lime juice, vinegar, cumin, and chili powder in a small bowl until well blended. Transfer rice to a large bowl and fluff with a fork. Mix in black beans, bell peppers, red onion, and chopped cilantro. Toss salad with dressing. Cover and refrigerate. (Can be prepared one day ahead.) Serve chilled or at room temperature.

Serves 6

Call (888) 887-3266 to confirm gluten-free status of Regina red wine vinegar.

Broccoli and Mushroom Salad

5   cups broccoli florets
1   large garlic clove, minced
⅓   cup extra virgin olive oil
¼   cup Heinz distilled white vinegar
1   tablespoon French's yellow mustard

2   tablespoons Domino light brown sugar
    Salt and freshly ground black pepper
6   ounces mushrooms, brushed under running water, and sliced

Place the broccoli in a 13 x 9-inch glass dish. In a medium bowl, combine the garlic, olive oil, vinegar, mustard, brown sugar, salt, and pepper. Whisk to combine. Pour the marinade over the broccoli. Refrigerate, covered, at least 6 hours or overnight. About 1 hour before serving, add mushrooms to the broccoli and chill until ready to serve.

Serves 6

Please go to the Consumer FAQs at heinz.com
to confirm the gluten-free status of Heinz Distilled White Vinegar.

Broccoli, Bacon, and Onion Salad

Salad:

4   cups broccoli florets
    (about 1 large bunch)
1   small red onion, chopped
    (about ¾ cup)

1   cup Diamond chopped walnuts
½   cup raisins
¼   pound Oscar Mayer bacon
    (4-5 slices)

Cut bacon slices in half and cook in large nonstick skillet over medium heat until brown and crisp. Transfer bacon to paper towels and drain. Combine broccoli, onion, walnuts, and raisins in a large salad bowl. Toss with dressing to coat. Crumble bacon on top of salad and chill about 4 hours. Mix in bacon just before serving. Serve chilled.

Dressing:

¾   cup Miracle Whip® or Hellmann's®
    mayonnaise
¼   cup sugar

1   tablespoon Heinz distilled white
    vinegar

To make dressing, mix mayonnaise, sugar, and vinegar in a small bowl.

Serves 6

Please go to the Consumer FAQs at heinz.com
to confirm the gluten-free status of Heinz Distilled White Vinegar.

Bean Salad

1 can (14½-ounce) Del Monte green beans

1 can (14½-ounce) Del Monte wax beans

1 can (16-ounce) Bush's dark red kidney beans

1 can (19-ounce) Progresso chick peas

1 small onion, sliced into rings

½ cup green pepper, chopped

⅔ cup sugar

⅓ cup extra light olive oil

⅔ cup Heinz apple cider vinegar

1 teaspoon salt

Freshly ground black pepper

Drain vegetables and combine with onion rings and green pepper in a large serving bowl. Combine sugar, oil, vinegar, salt, and pepper and pour over bean mixture. Refrigerate at least 12 hours before serving.

Serves 10

Please go to the Consumer FAQs at heinz.com to confirm the gluten-free status of Heinz Apple Cider Vinegar. Please note that Heinz Apple Cider Flavored Vinegar is not gluten-free.

Cole Slaw

½ green bell pepper, cleaned and quartered

1 green onion, coarsely chopped

1 medium carrot, peeled and chopped

½ cabbage head

½ cup Kraft Miracle Whip® or Hellmann's® or Best Foods® Real Mayonnaise

Freshly ground black pepper

1 tablespoon sugar

½ teaspoon McCormick lemon pepper seasoning

1 tablespoon Heinz distilled white vinegar

Using a food processor, gently process the bell pepper, onion, and carrot being careful not to over process. Cut ½ of the cabbage into chunks and place in the food processor. Process lightly, making sure the cabbage doesn't become mushy. Slice the remaining cabbage thinly. Mix the cabbage together with the processed vegetables. In a separate bowl, mix the remaining ingredients together and allow to stand for a few minutes. Combine the mayonnaise mixture with the vegetables and toss. Chill for 1 hour.

Serves 6

Please go to the Consumer FAQs at heinz.com to
confirm the gluten-free status of Heinz Distilled White Vinegar.

Egg Salad

4   hard-cooked eggs, chopped
1   tablespoon chopped sweet onion
3   tablespoons mayonnaise or salad
    dressing (such as Miracle Whip®)

Edward & Sons onion and garlic
crackers, for serving

Combine chopped eggs and onion. Blend in mayonnaise. Serve on crackers.

Serves 4

Potato Salad

4   large baking potatoes
    (about 3 pounds)
¼   cup Heinz distilled white vinegar
2   tablespoons vegetable oil
2   large hard-cooked eggs, chopped
1   cup chopped celery

1   medium Vidalia onion, chopped
¾   cup Hellmann's® or Best Foods®
    Real Mayonnaise
1   teaspoon salt
    Freshly ground black pepper

In a 6-quart saucepan, cover potatoes with cold, salted water by 2 inches and simmer uncovered until just tender, 35 to 40 minutes depending on size. Drain in a colander and cool slightly, about 20 minutes.

While potatoes are cooling, whisk together vinegar and oil in a large bowl. When potatoes are just cool enough to handle, peel and cut into 1-inch pieces, adding to oil and vinegar mixture as cut. Toss gently with a rubber spatula to combine. Let cool to room temperature, then add eggs, celery, onion, mayonnaise, salt, and pepper. Stir gently to combine. Chill 4 to 6 hours, or overnight.

Serves 8

Please go to the Consumer FAQs at heinz.com to
confirm the gluten-free status of Heinz Distilled White Vinegar.

Grilled Cheese and Pepperoni Sandwich

2   slices Kinnikinnick Italian White
    Tapioca Rice Bread
2   slices mozzarella cheese (such as
    Kraft Deli Deluxe)

5   pieces Hormel pepperoni
1   tablespoon butter

Spread each slice of bread with butter. Place buttered sides together and set on a plate. Top bread with one slice of cheese, arrange pepperoni slices on top and cover with second slice of cheese. Lift top sandwich bread slice with toppings and place in nonstick pan over medium heat, or in electric skillet. Immediately cover with bottom slice of bread, making sure butter is on the outside of the sandwich. Grill bottom of sandwich, then flip carefully to grill second side.

Serves 1

Kinnikinnick products may be ordered at
www.goglutenfree.com or call (877) 503-4466.

Hot Corned Beef Sandwiches

4   slices Kinnikinnick Italian White
    Tapioca Rice Bread, lightly toasted
2   tablespoons Maille Dijon style
    mustard

8   slices Dietz and Watson corned beef
4   slices Sargento Deli Style Sliced
    Baby Swiss Cheese

Spread one side of each toast slice with mustard. Arrange 4 toasts on a baking sheet and divide corned beef among them. Top corned beef with cheese and broil under broiler about 4 inches from heat until cheese is melted.

Serves 2

Please visit www.dietzandwatson.com to determine the gluten-free status of Dietz and Watson corned beef. Go to www.sargentocheese.com to determine the gluten-free status of Sargento Swiss cheese. Kinnikinnick products can be ordered at www.goglutenfree.com or call (877) 503-4466.

Peanut Butter & Jelly Waffle Sandwich

1   tablespoon Dickinson's Pure
    Seedless Cascade Mountain Red
    Raspberry Preserves

1   tablespoon Simply Jif creamy
    peanut butter
2   Van's wheat-free mini waffles

Toast waffles on light or lowest toaster setting and cool slightly. Spread one waffle with peanut butter and one with jelly. Put together and serve whole, or break into four mini sandwiches. Serve with milk.

Serves 1

To avoid cross contamination, a separate toaster should be
used for gluten-free foods. A toaster oven, where the rack can be removed
and washed if others have used it may be a good alternative.

Bacon, Lettuce & Tomato Sandwich

2   slices Oscar Mayer bacon, crisply
    cooked
2   slices Kinnikinnick Italian White
    Tapioca Rice Bread

2   slices tomato
1   leaf lettuce
1   tablespoon mayonnaise or salad
    dressing (such as Miracle Whip®)

Toast bread in toaster. Place bacon on one slice of bread. Top with tomato and lettuce. Spread second slice of bread with Miracle Whip and place on top of lettuce.

Serves 1

Kinnikinnick products may be ordered
at www.goglutenfree.com or call (877) 503-4466.

MAIN
COURSES

Main Courses

Beef Brisket

1	large size Reynolds Oven Bag (16 x 17½-inch)	1	envelope Lipton Recipe Secrets onion soup mix
1	(3½-pound) center cut beef brisket	½	cup water
	Salt and freshly ground black pepper	5	medium red potatoes, quartered
2	tablespoons vegetable oil	6	carrots, quartered
		1	medium onion, quartered

Preheat oven to 325°. Place bag in 13 x 9-inch roasting pan with opening towards wide side of pan. Pat brisket dry and season with salt and pepper. Heat oil in a 6 to 8-quart wide heavy pot over medium heat, then brown meat well on all sides, about 10 minutes total. Transfer beef to bag and sprinkle with onion soup mix. Add water along sides of beef. Place potatoes, carrots, and onion around beef. Close oven bag with nylon tie. Cut six ½-inch slits in top of bag to allow steam to escape. Tuck ends of bag in pan. Bake in middle of oven until meat is very tender, 3 to 3½ hours. Slice meat across the grain into ¼-inch thick slices.

Serves 8

Beef Stew

1   envelope Lipton Recipe Secrets Onion Soup Mix

2   tablespoons tapioca flour (Such as Bob's Red Mill)

     Freshly ground black pepper

1½ pounds lean beef stew meat

2   tablespoons vegetable oil

32 ounces Kitchen Basics beef stock

6   medium carrots, quartered

5   small new potatoes, quartered

3   medium onions, quartered

In a shallow bowl, mix soup mix, tapioca flour, and black pepper. Dredge beef in soup mixture and brown the beef on all sides in vegetable oil over medium heat. Add beef stock and bring to a boil. Reduce heat to low; cover and simmer 60 minutes. Add carrots, potatoes, and onions. Simmer for 45 minutes.

Serves 6

Crock Pot Beef Stew

2 pounds beef stew meat
1 tablespoon vegetable oil
1 envelope Fantastic Foods Onion
   Soup & Recipe Mix
1 teaspoon salt
   Freshly ground black pepper
1 tablespoon Minute tapioca

1 tablespoon sugar
6 medium carrots, quartered
3 medium onions, quartered
5 small new potatoes, quartered
1 (28-ounce) can Del Monte ready cut
   tomatoes, undrained

Brown meat in vegetable oil in large stockpot. Place browned meat in bottom of crock pot. Sprinkle with onion soup mix, salt, pepper, tapioca, and sugar. Add carrots, onions, and potatoes. Pour tomatoes over the top. Cover; bake on low for 6-8 hours.

Serves 6

Filet Mignon Roast

3   large baking potatoes (about 3 pounds), cut into 1-inch pieces

1   teaspoon olive oil

Salt and freshly ground black pepper

3½ pounds beef tenderloin

Preheat oven to 500°. Toss potatoes with oil and season with salt and freshly ground black pepper. Arrange in a single layer in the bottom of a nonstick roasting pan. Season tenderloin with salt and freshly ground black pepper. Insert meat thermometer into thickest portion of tenderloin. Add tenderloin to roasting pan, nestling it into potato mixture. Bake at 500° for 30 to 45 minutes or until thermometer registers 145° (medium-rare) to 160° (medium), stirring potatoes once. Place tenderloin and potatoes on a serving platter and cover with foil. Let stand 10 minutes before carving.

Serves 6

Pennsylvania Pot Roast

Roast:

2   tablespoons vegetable oil
1   (2½-pound) beef eye of round roast
    Freshly ground black pepper
8   ounces beef stock (such as Kitchen Basics)
2   medium onions, chopped
½   cup Del Monte diced tomatoes, undrained

1   medium carrot, chopped
1   celery rib, chopped
¼   cup chopped turnip (cut in ½-inch cubes)
¼   teaspoon McCormick thyme leaves
1   bay leaf (such as McCormick)
6   small red potatoes

Heat oil in a large Dutch oven over medium-high heat until hot. Add roast, browning on all sides. Season beef with freshly ground black pepper. Add beef stock, onion, tomatoes, carrot, celery, turnip, thyme, and bay leaf to pan; bring to a boil. Cover, reduce heat to low, and simmer 2½ hours or until tender. Scrub potatoes and cut in half. Put in pot of salted water and bring to a boil. Boil 15 minutes, then put in Dutch oven with pot roast and simmer for an additional 30 minutes. Remove roast and potatoes. Slice roast; place on a serving platter with potatoes. Cover and keep warm while making gravy.

Gravy:

2   tablespoons Bob's Red Mill potato starch

2   tablespoons water

To make gravy, combine potato starch and water in a small bowl. Whisk until smooth. Stir into remaining juices in the Dutch oven. Simmer gravy, stirring occasionally, until gravy reaches the desired consistency, about 10 minutes. Discard bay leaf. Serve gravy with roast.

Serves 6

Pot Roast

Roast:

3½ pounds boneless beef rump roast, tied

Salt and freshly ground black pepper

4 medium potatoes, peeled

8 medium carrots, peeled and quartered

2 medium onions

Position a rack in the center of the oven. Preheat the oven to 300°. Season roast on all sides with salt and pepper. Place the roast, fat side up, in a roasting pan and add about ½-inch of water. Cover. Roast at 300°, for 2 hours. Add potatoes, carrots, and onions and roast for 1 hour more. Remove vegetables and roast, peel fat off and cut cords. Let roast stand for 10 to 15 minutes before carving.

Gravy:

3 cups water

¼ cup cornstarch

Salt and freshly ground black pepper

Meanwhile, prepare gravy. In a small bowl, combine cornstarch with water. Whisk until cornstarch is dissolved. Add salt and pepper. Add cornstarch mixture to remaining juices in roasting pan and simmer over medium heat on stovetop. Cook, whisking or stirring, until gravy comes to a boil and thickens slightly. Strain through a fine-mesh sieve, if desired, and serve hot.

Serves 6

Beef Kabobs

1½ pounds trimmed sirloin steak, cut into 1-inch cubes

2 tablespoons extra virgin olive oil

1½ tablespoons Stonewall Kitchen balsamic vinegar

¼ teaspoon McCormick oregano leaves

2 cloves garlic

Freshly ground black pepper

8 cherry tomatoes

1 medium red onion, cut into quarters

8 large mushroom caps, brushed clean

1 medium red bell pepper, cut into 2-inch pieces

1 medium zucchini, cut crosswise into slices ½-inch thick

3 cups cooked rice, for serving

To make marinade, mix the oil, vinegar, oregano, garlic, and pepper in a bowl. Place meat in an a large Ziploc bag and pour the marinade over the meat. Seal bag and turn so that all pieces are coated. Refrigerate for 1-4 hours. Turn the meat once while marinating. Remove the meat from the marinade and discard marinade. Thread kabobs, beginning with a piece of meat. Alternate pieces of meat with pieces of vegetables, ending with any extra pieces of meat. Preheat the grill. Set skewers on the grill and cook, covered, turning half way through cooking time. Beef kabobs will take about 20 minutes to cook. Serve with rice.

Serves 4

Please go to www.stonewallkitchen.com to confirm gluten-free status of the balsamic vinegar. Stonewall Kitchen products may be ordered at www.stonewallkitchen.com or call (800) 207-5267.

Grammy's Chili

2 tablespoons vegetable oil

1 whole Vidalia onion, chopped

6 whole celery stalks, chopped

1 medium yellow bell pepper, chopped

3 cloves garlic, minced

2 pounds ground sirloin, browned and drained

1 (28-ounce) can Del Monte diced tomatoes, undrained

1 (8-ounce) can Hunt's tomato paste

1 (5.5-ounce) can V-8® vegetable juice

2 tablespoons McCormick chili powder

2 tablespoons McCormick paprika

2 teaspoons McCormick allspice

2 (19-ounce) cans Progresso (or Bush's) Dark Red kidney beans, drained

8 ounces Cheddar cheese (such as Heluva® Good), shredded (2 cups)

In a large stockpot, heat the oil over medium heat. Add the onion, celery, bell pepper, and garlic and cook and stir for 10 minutes. Add the browned meat, tomatoes, tomato paste, and V-8 juice. Sprinkle with chili powder, paprika, and allspice. Stir to combine. Simmer, covered, 1 to 2 hours, stirring occasionally. Add kidney beans 1 hour before serving. Ladle chili into individual bowls and garnish with grated cheese.

Serves 12

This recipe from my mother-in-law will be the best chili you have ever made.

Crock-Pot Chili

1	pound ground sirloin	¼	teaspoon salt
1	cup chopped onion	1	garlic clove, minced
½	cup chopped green bell pepper	1	(15-ounce) can kidney beans (such as Progresso or Bush's), undrained
¼	cup water		
1	tablespoon McCormick chili powder	1	(14.5-ounce) can Del Monte diced tomatoes, undrained
1	teaspoon sugar	4	ounces Cheddar cheese (such as Heluva® Good), shredded (1 cup)
1	teaspoon McCormick ground cumin		

Cook the ground sirloin in a large skillet over medium heat until brown, stirring to crumble. Add chopped onion, bell pepper, water, chili powder, sugar, cumin, salt, and garlic and cook for 7 minutes or until onion is tender. Place meat mixture in a Crock-Pot; stir in beans and tomatoes. Cover with lid and cook on low-heat setting for 4 hours. Spoon into bowls; sprinkle with cheese.

Serves 6

Hamburger Casserole

1   pound ground beef
2   medium potatoes, peeled and cut
    crosswise into ¼-inch-thick slices
1   medium sweet onion, chopped
2   cups sliced carrots (¼-inch-thick)

1½ cups cooked rice
1   (28-ounce) can Del Monte diced
    tomatoes, undrained
    Salt and freshly ground black pepper

Brown ground beef and drain excess fat. Layer ingredients in a greased 3-quart baking dish in the following order: potatoes, onions, ground beef, carrots, rice and tomatoes. Season with salt and pepper. Bake at 300° for 1 hour.

Serves 6

This is an easy recipe using leftover rice.

Hobo Dinners

1 pound ground beef, pinched into
   1-inch pieces

4 medium potatoes, peeled and cut
   into long, thin wedges

4 medium carrots, peeled and sliced
   lengthwise

1 medium onion, peeled and sliced
   into thin rings

   Salt, pepper, and garlic powder

4 tablespoons Heinz ketchup

Preheat oven to 400°. Tear off 4 sheets of heavy-duty aluminum foil (about 18 x 20 inches). Layer the vegetables on each sheet, starting with the potatoes, then carrots, and onions. Pinch ground beef into bite-size pieces and add on top of vegetables. Season with salt, pepper, and garlic powder. Spoon 1 tablespoon ketchup over the top. Pull foil up over the top of each bundle and crimp the edges to seal. Place on a cookie sheet. Bake 45 to 60 minutes or to desired doneness. May also be baked on a grill or in a campfire.

Serves 4

My son, Andrew, learned this recipe when he attended
Camp Celiac in North Scituate, Rhode Island. Please go to the Consumer FAQs
at heinz.com to confirm the gluten-free status of Heinz Ketchup.

Stuffed Peppers

4	medium green or red bell peppers	1	pound ground sirloin
4	medium potatoes, peeled and cubed (½-inch cubes)	1	can (28 ounces) Del Monte ready cut tomatoes, undrained
1	medium onion, chopped	1	can (11 ounces) Green Giant Niblets corn, drained
1	tablespoon vegetable oil		

Preheat oven to 350°. Remove top and seeds from bell peppers. Discard stems, chop pepper tops, and set aside. Parboil peppers for 5 minutes, drain. Parboil cubed potatoes about 10 minutes, drain. In a small nonstick skillet, heat the olive oil over low heat. Add the onion and cook, stirring frequently, until the onion is soft and translucent, about 10 minutes.

Brown meat in a large nonstick skillet; drain fat. Add the onion, tomatoes, corn, reserved chopped green pepper, and cooked potatoes. Mix well. Stand peppers upright in a 3-quart baking dish, and stuff with meat and vegetable mixture, lightly packing mixture inside peppers and all around sides. Cover and bake for 45 minutes.

Serves 4

Select peppers that are flat on the bottom so they will stand up better while cooking.

Texas Hash

1 large onion, chopped
1 medium green bell pepper, chopped
1½ tablespoons vegetable oil
1 pound ground beef, extra lean
1 can (14.5 ounces) Del Monte diced
   tomatoes

1 can (11 ounces) Green Giant
   Niblets corn, drained
¾ teaspoon McCormick chili powder
¼ teaspoon salt
   Freshly ground black pepper
½ cup water
2 cups cooked rice

Heat oil in a large, deep, covered skillet over medium heat. Add onions and green pepper and cook, stirring frequently, until the onion is soft and translucent, about 10 minutes. Add meat and cook until there is no pink color left, stirring with a fork to break up the meat. Add tomatoes, corn, chili powder, salt, pepper, water, and rice. Cover and simmer 5 minutes.

Serves 4

This would be a good meal for a weekend camping trip.

Wild Rice Baron

4	cups water	2	pounds lean ground beef
2	cups wild rice		Freshly ground black pepper
2	teaspoons salt	2	cups Breakstone's sour cream
½	cup (1 stick) butter	¼	cup San-J Tamari wheat free soy sauce
1	medium onion, chopped		
½	cup celery, chopped	½	cup slivered almonds, save some for garnish
1	pound fresh mushrooms, sliced		

Bring water to a boil in a 2-quart heavy saucepan, then add rice and 1 teaspoon salt. Reduce heat to low and cook, covered, until rice is tender and most grains are split open, about 1 hour (not all liquid will be absorbed). Drain if necessary. Melt butter in a large nonstick skillet over moderate heat, then cook onion, celery, and mushrooms, stirring, until softened, about 8 minutes. Transfer vegetables to a large bowl. Add ground beef to the skillet and brown over medium heat; drain fat. Season with pepper. In a large bowl, combine sour cream, soy sauce, and remaining 1 teaspoon salt. Add cooked wild rice, beef, vegetable mixture, and almonds. Toss lightly. Place mixture in lightly greased 3-quart baking dish. Bake at 350° for about an hour, covered. Stir several times and add water if needed. Garnish with reserved almonds.

Serves 8

Wild rice is not actually rice, but a long-grain marsh grass native
to the northern Great Lakes region. It has a nutty flavor and chewy texture.

Meat Loaf

1 pound ground beef	¼ cup whole milk
¼ pound ground pork	½ cup sweet onion, chopped
¼ pound ground veal	1 medium zucchini, shredded
1 large egg	¼ cup Heinz ketchup

Preheat oven to 350°. Mix meat in large mixing bowl. Add egg, milk, onion, zucchini, and ketchup and combine. Mix well and shape into a loaf shape. Place meat loaf in a shallow baking dish. Bake for 60 minutes. Remove from oven and insert meat thermometer. Drain fat and return to oven until thermometer measures 177°F, about 10 minutes.

Serves 6

Please go to the Consumer FAQs at heinz.com
to confirm the gluten-free status of Heinz Ketchup.

Franks and Beans

3	Hebrew National beef hot dogs, sliced ⅓-inch thick	1	jar (18 ounces) B & M baked beans

Slice hot dogs and brown in a large nonstick skillet over medium heat. Reduce heat to low, add baked beans and simmer for 5 minutes, stirring occasionally.

Serves 2

Tacos

1   pound ground sirloin
2   tablespoons Old El Paso mild taco
     seasoning mix
½   cup water
12   taco shells (such as Old El Paso)
½   cup Green Mountain Gringo salsa

2   ounces Cheddar or Colby/Jack
     Heluva® Good cheese, shredded
     (½ cup)
¾   cup shredded iceberg lettuce
1   medium tomato, chopped

Brown ground sirloin in a large skillet over medium heat. Add taco seasoning and water. Simmer 10 to 15 minutes or until thick. Prepare taco shells according to package directions. Spoon ¼ cup beef mixture into each taco shell. Top each with salsa, cheese, tomato, and lettuce.

Serves 4

Patty Melt

4 slices Kinnikinnick Italian White
   Tapioca Rice Bread

1 tablespoon butter, softened

4 slices Swiss cheese (such as Kraft)

½ tablespoon olive oil

1 small onion, peeled and sliced into
   rings

2 ground chuck patties (¼ pound
   each), grilled

Spread each slice of bread with butter. Heat a medium nonstick skillet over medium heat. Place bread slices on pan (butter sides down). Top each slice of bread with a slice of cheese. Grill until bread is lightly browned and cheese is melted. Heat olive oil in a small nonstick skillet, add onions and grill until caramelized. Assemble patty melt by placing grilled patties over one slice of toast, top with caramelized onions and remaining slice toast.

Serves 2

Kinnikinnick products can be ordered
at www.goglutenfree.com or call (877) 503-4466.

Hamburger Kabobs

1	pound ground beef chuck			Freshly ground black pepper
1	egg white		1	medium red onion, cut into quarters
1	tablespoon Heinz ketchup		8	cherry tomatoes
½	teaspoon salt			Potato chips for serving
¼	teaspoon McCormick garlic powder			

Place meat in a mixing bowl. Stir in egg white, ketchup, salt, and garlic powder. Season with freshly ground pepper. Mix thoroughly. Shape hamburger into 1½-inch balls. Thread double-prong skewers with hamburgers, onion, and cherry tomatoes. Preheat the grill. Set skewers on grill and cook about 8 to 10 minutes, rotating every 2 minutes. Serve with potato chips.

Serves 4

A fun way to eat hamburgers without the buns. Use double-prong skewers to hold the hamburgers on the skewer while grilling.

Shish Kabobs

¾ pound trimmed sirloin steak, cut into 1-inch cubes

1 pound chicken breast, cut into 1-inch cubes

⅓ cup extra virgin olive oil

¼ cup white wine vinegar

½ teaspoon McCormick oregano leaves

3 cloves garlic
Freshly ground black pepper

12 cherry tomato

1 medium red onion, cut in quarters

12 large mushroom caps, brushed clean

1 medium red bell pepper, cut into 2-inch pieces

1 medium green bell pepper, cut into 2-inch pieces

3 cups cooked rice, for serving

To make marinade, mix the oil, vinegar, oregano, pepper and garlic in a bowl. Place chicken in 1 gallon-size Ziploc bag and beef in another. Pour half the marinade over each. Toss so that all pieces are coated. Refrigerate for 1-4 hours. Turn the meat once while marinating. Thread skewers, beginning with a piece of meat. Alternate pieces of meat with pieces of vegetables, ending with any extra pieces of meat. Make 3 kabobs with chicken and vegetables and 3 kabobs with beef. Preheat the grill. Set skewers on the grill and cook, turning half way through cooking time. Chicken kabobs will take about 25 minutes and beef kabobs about 20 minutes. Serve with rice.

Serves 4

Stir-Fried Beef with Mushrooms and Sugar Snap Peas

1 pound sirloin steak, sliced into thin strips, 2-inch long

8 ounces fresh mushrooms, sliced

1 cup sugar snap peas

½ cup finely chopped sweet onion

4 slices ginger root, minced fine

2 cloves garlic, minced or pressed

1 tablespoon Argo cornstarch

2 tablespoons Holland House sherry cooking wine

2 tablespoons San-J Tamari wheat free soy sauce

3 tablespoons light olive oil

½ cup Kitchen Basics beef stock

3 cups cooked rice, for serving

To make the sauce, combine the sherry cooking wine, soy sauce, and cornstarch in a small bowl. Whisk to dissolve the cornstarch. Set aside. In a wok, heat 1 tablespoon oil over medium-high heat, swirling to coat the bottom and sides. Add ginger root, garlic, and onion and stir and toss a few times. Add 1-half of the beef and stir and toss until browned but still slightly pink inside, about 2 to 3 minutes. Transfer beef to a shallow bowl. Add another 1 tablespoon oil to the wok, and cook the remaining beef in the same manner. Transfer second batch of beef to the shallow bowl. Add remaining 1 tablespoon oil to the wok. Add mushrooms, sugar snap peas, and onion. Stir and toss to coat with oil. Reduce heat to medium and stir in beef stock. Cook, covered, until vegetables are nearly done, about 2 minutes. Return beef to wok. Quickly whisk the reserved sauce and add it to the wok. Stir and toss until the sauce begins to thicken, about 1 minute. Serve immediately over rice.

Serves 4

"When serving stir-fried dishes, it is well to remember an old Chinese proverb which says: It is better that a man wait for his meal, than the meal wait for the man."

~ *The Thousand Recipe Chinese Cookbook*

Stir-Fry Beef with Asparagus

2   teaspoons cornstarch
3   tablespoons water
3   tablespoons San-J Tamari wheat-
      free soy sauce
1   teaspoon finely chopped, peeled
      fresh ginger
1   small clove garlic, minced or pressed
1   medium green onion, finely
      chopped

⅛   teaspoon red pepper flakes
1   pound asparagus, cut diagonally
      into 1½-inch pieces
2   tablespoons extra light olive oil
1   pound sirloin steak, sliced into thin
      strips 2-inch long
1   medium red bell pepper, cut into
      thin strips
    Steamed rice, for serving

In a small bowl, dissolve cornstarch in water. Add tamari sauce, ginger, garlic, green onion, and red pepper flakes. Set aside. In a covered microwave-safe baking dish, microwave asparagus on High (100% power), 4 minutes. In a wok over high heat, heat 1 tablespoon of the oil, swirling to coat the bottom and sides of the wok. When the oil is very hot, but not quite smoking, add half the beef strips and stir and toss until lightly browned but still slightly pink inside, 2 to 3 minutes. Transfer to a bowl. Add the remaining 1 tablespoon oil to the pan and cook the remaining beef in the same manner. Return the first batch of beef to the pan. Add the bell pepper and stir and toss over high heat until just beginning to wilt, 1 to 2 minutes. Quickly stir in the reserved sauce. Cook, tossing the mixture occasionally until the sauce thickens. Add the asparagus to the pan, toss to coat evenly with the sauce and serve immediately.

Serves 4

To make the beef easier to slice, partially freeze the beef for 10 to 20 minutes.

Brunswick Stew

2½ pounds chicken breast halves

1 (14.5 ounce) can Del Monte Petite Cut Diced Tomatoes

1 (14.75-ounce) can Green Giant cream style sweet corn

1 cup Heinz ketchup

½ cup barbecue sauce (such as Sweet Baby Ray's)

1 onion, chopped

1 tablespoon Heinz distilled white vinegar

1 tablespoon Lea & Perrins Worcestershire sauce

Salt and freshly ground black pepper

Cooked rice, for serving

Place the chicken in a large pot filled with enough water to cover the chicken. Bring to a boil. Reduce heat and simmer, uncovered, 25 minutes. Remove from heat, let stand, uncovered, 20 minutes. Reserve 1 cup of stock. Transfer chicken to a cutting board and cool, about 5 minutes. Remove the skin and bones and chop meat. In a separate pot, mix the chicken and remaining ingredients. Add reserved stock and simmer for 30 minutes, stirring often to prevent sticking. Serve stew over rice.

Serves 6

Please go to the Consumer FAQs at heinz.com to
confirm the gluten-free status of Heinz Distilled White Vinegar.

Roast Chicken with Gravy

Chicken:

1	(6- to 7-pound) roasting chicken	4	sprigs fresh rosemary
2	medium onions, peeled and sliced ½-inch thick	2	tablespoons unsalted butter Coarse salt and freshly ground black pepper
1	medium lemon		
3	garlic cloves, peeled		

Heat oven to 425°. Remove the giblets from the chicken cavity. Rinse the chicken inside and out under cold running water. Dry the chicken with paper towels. In the center of a heavy-duty roasting pan, arrange onion slices in two rows, touching. Roll lemon on countertop to soften and pierce the entire surface of the lemon with a fork. Using the side of a large knife, gently press on the garlic cloves to crush slightly. Insert garlic, rosemary, and lemon into cavity. Place chicken in pan, on onion slices. Cross chicken legs and tie together with kitchen twine.

Soften butter in microwave for 15 seconds on high. Spread the softened butter over the entire surface of the chicken to ensure even browning. Season with salt and freshly ground pepper. Roast until skin is deep golden brown and crisp and the juices run clear when pierced, about 1½ hours. An instant-read thermometer inserted into the breast should read 180 °. Remove the chicken from the oven, and transfer to a serving platter. Let the chicken stand at room temperature for 10 to 15 minutes to redistribute the juices throughout the chicken.

Gravy:

1   cup Kitchen Basics chicken stock

Remove the onions from the roasting pan and pour the pan drippings into a shallow bowl. Using a large spoon, skim off and discard as much of the fat as possible. To make the gravy, pour the remaining drippings back into the roasting pan. Place the pan on the stove, over medium-high heat, and cook for about 1 minute. Add chicken stock and raise the heat to high. Using a wooden spoon, deglaze the pan by stirring up any baked-on brown bits that are stuck on the bottom so that they combine with the stock. Cook until the liquid is reduced by half, about 4 minutes. Pour the gravy through a strainer into a serving bowl.

Roast Chicken with Potatoes and Bell Peppers

2   packages (3 pounds each) Perdue Oven Stuffer Half Roasters

4   fresh rosemary sprigs

4   medium new potatoes, quartered

3   tablespoons extra virgin olive oil
    Salt and freshly ground black pepper

1   whole yellow bell pepper, cored and quartered lengthwise

1   whole orange bell pepper, cored and quartered lengthwise

Preheat oven to 400°. Rinse chicken with cold water and pat dry. Set chicken in a roasting pan just large enough to hold it and potatoes in one layer. Add rosemary to pan, tucking it under chicken. Arrange potatoes around chicken and drizzle with oil. Season with salt and pepper. Stir to coat potatoes with oil. Roast chicken uncovered for 30 minutes.

Remove chicken from oven and turn potatoes over. Tip pan and baste chicken and potatoes. Add peppers to pan; push them under potatoes and chicken. Roast 15 to 30 minutes more, or until potatoes are tender and chicken juices run clear when thickest part is pierced with a thin knife or skewer. Transfer chicken to a cutting board and cover loosely with foil. If potatoes are not yet tender, bake potatoes a few more minutes. Serve chicken with roasted peppers and potatoes.

Serves 6

Chicken with Garlic Rosemary Citrus Sauce

1   package (about 1 pound) thin-sliced   1   tablespoon extra light olive oil
    skinless and boneless chicken   ½   cup Stonewall Kitchen Garlic
    breast   Rosemary Citrus sauce

In a large nonstick skillet, heat oil and cook chicken over medium heat until browned and cooked through, about 10 minutes. Stir in sauce. Reduce heat to low. Cover and simmer 20 to 35 minutes until chicken is tender, stirring occasionally.

Serves 4

Please go to www.stonewallkitchen.com to
confirm gluten-free status of sauce. Stonewall Kitchen products may
be ordered at www.stonewallkitchen.com or call (800) 207-5267.

Chicken with Lemon Sauce

½ teaspoon salt
Freshly ground black pepper
½ teaspoon McCormick allspice, divided
4 skinless boneless chicken breast halves
2½ tablespoons olive oil

¼ cup dry white wine
½ cup Kitchen Basics chicken stock
1½ tablespoons fresh lemon juice, divided
1 teaspoon grated lemon peel
1 tablespoon minced shallot
¼ teaspoon McCormick thyme

Mix salt, pepper, and ¼ teaspoon allspice in small bowl. Rub spice mixture over both sides of chicken. In a large nonstick skillet, heat 1 tablespoon oil over medium heat. Add chicken and cook and stir until cooked through.

Transfer chicken to platter, tent with foil to keep warm. Add wine to skillet and bring to boil. Stir in chicken stock, ½ tablespoon lemon juice, and lemon peel. Boil until reduced slightly. Whisk in shallots, thyme, 1½ tablespoons oil, 1 tablespoon lemon juice, and ¼ teaspoon allspice. Heat to boiling. Pour sauce over chicken and serve.

Serves 4

Chicken with Onions

¼ cup fresh lime juice
3 cloves garlic, minced
1 teaspoon crushed red pepper
1 teaspoon salt
  Freshly ground black pepper

1 pound skinless and boneless chicken breasts
2 large onions, thinly sliced
1 tablespoon extra light olive oil
3 cups cooked rice, for serving

Preheat oven to 450°. In a small bowl, combine lime juice, garlic, crushed red pepper, salt, and pepper. Place chicken and onions in a 1 gallon Ziploc bag; pour marinade over chicken and seal bag. Marinate in refrigerator 2 hours, turning occasionally.

In a Dutch oven, heat oil over medium-high heat. Remove chicken breasts from plastic bag, and add to pan; cook 2 minutes on each side or until browned. Remove pan from heat. Add onion slices from plastic bag to Dutch Oven. Using tongs, arrange chicken pieces so they are nestled on onion slices. Bake, uncovered, at 450° for 20 minutes.

Remove chicken from pan; stir onion slices, scraping bottom of pan to loosen browned bits. Return chicken to pan; reduce oven temperature to 375° and bake an additional 15 minutes. Place ½ cup rice on each serving plate and top with chicken and onion mixture.

Serves 4

Cornflake Chicken Chops

1	pound thin sliced chicken breasts	1	large egg, lightly beaten
1	tablespoon cornstarch (such as Argo)	1	cup Nature's Path Fruit Juice Sweet Corn Flakes, chopped in blender
½	teaspoon salt	1	tablespoon extra light olive oil
	Freshly ground black pepper	1	tablespoon butter

Place chicken in a medium bowl. Sprinkle with cornstarch and season with salt and pepper. Dip chicken in egg and dredge in cornflakes, turning to coat completely. Heat oil and butter in a nonstick skillet over medium heat. Add chicken and cook, about 8 to 10 minutes on each side, until chicken is cooked through.

Serves 4

Glorified Chicken

1   tablespoon extra light olive oil
1½ pounds thin sliced chicken breasts

1   can (18 ounces) Progresso Creamy
    Mushroom soup
¼   teaspoon McCormick thyme

In skillet, heat oil and cook chicken over medium heat until browned, about 10 minutes. Simmer soup in saucepan over medium heat for 10 minutes while browning chicken. Add soup and thyme to chicken. Reduce heat to low. Cover and simmer 20 to 35 minutes until chicken is tender, stirring occasionally.

Serves 4

Orange-Dijon Chicken

1   pound skinless and boneless chicken breasts

1½ tablespoons extra light olive oil

1   tablespoon butter

    Salt and freshly ground black pepper

4   tablespoons orange marmalade (such as Smucker's)

2   tablespoons Maille Dijon style mustard

    Hot cooked rice, for accompaniment

In a small bowl, combine marmalade and mustard. Melt oil and butter in a large skillet over medium heat. Add chicken and cook about 2 minutes, turning to brown evenly. Season with salt and freshly ground pepper. Reduce heat to medium and spread marmalade sauce over chicken. Simmer until chicken is cooked through, about 15 minutes.

Serves 4

Rockin' Chicken

3   cloves garlic, minced
2   tablespoons extra light olive oil
1   teaspoon McCormick ground cumin
1   teaspoon McCormick ground ginger
½   teaspoon coarse salt
½   teaspoon McCormick paprika

Freshly ground black pepper
1½ pounds chicken thighs, boneless and skinless
1   teaspoon freshly grated lemon peel
3   cups cooked rice, for serving

Combine garlic, cumin, ginger, salt, paprika, pepper, and lemon peel in a medium bowl. Transfer to a 1 gallon Ziploc bag. Add the chicken pieces and coat them well with the mixture. Refrigerate for 30 minutes. Heat oil in a Dutch oven on the stovetop over medium heat. Add chicken. Cook for about 2 minutes, turning to brown evenly. Cover and cook 10 minutes. Turn the chicken pieces over and cook another 10 minutes. Serve immediately.

Serves 4

Chicken Enchilada Casserole

3 cups cooked chicken, chopped

8 ounces Cheddar cheese (such as Heluva® Good), shredded (2 cups)

1 can (14½ ounces) Del Monte diced tomatoes

1 large onion, chopped

4 ounces Old El Paso chopped green chiles

½ teaspoon McCormick Hot Mexican-style chili powder

8 (6-inch) Mission white corn tortillas

⅓ cup Ortega mild taco sauce

8 ounces Monterey Jack cheese (such as Heluva® Good), shredded (2 cups)

Preheat oven to 350°. In a medium bowl, combine chicken, Cheddar cheese, tomato, onion, green chiles, and chili powder. Arrange 3 tortillas in bottom of a buttered 11 x 7-inch baking dish. Spread half of the chicken mixture over tortillas. Repeat procedure with 3 tortillas and remaining chicken mixture. Top with remaining 2 tortillas. Spread taco sauce over tortillas; sprinkle with Monterey Jack cheese. Bake at 350° for 20 to 30 minutes or until cheese melts.

Serves 4

Coq Au Vin

1 tablespoon Argo cornstarch
1 teaspoon McCormick paprika
½ teaspoon salt
 Freshly ground black pepper
1½ pounds boneless, skinless chicken breasts
1 tablespoon olive oil
1¼ cups Kitchen Basics chicken stock
½ cup white wine

1 teaspoon McCormick thyme leaves
1 teaspoon McCormick rosemary leaves
5 cloves garlic, crushed
1 pound carrots, chopped
4 medium red or Yukon Gold potatoes, quartered
1 medium sweet onion, quartered
8 ounces mushrooms, stems removed

Combine cornstarch, paprika, salt, and pepper in a large Ziploc bag. Add chicken pieces to bag. Seal and shake to coat.

Heat oil in a large nonstick skillet over medium heat. Add chicken pieces and cook 5 minutes on each side or until browned. Remove chicken from skillet; place in shallow roasting pan.

Add chicken stock, white wine, thyme, rosemary, and garlic to skillet. Cook over medium heat 1 minute, scraping bottom of skillet to loosen browned bits. Remove from heat; set aside.

Arrange carrots, potato, onions, and mushrooms around chicken in roasting pan. Pour chicken stock mixture over chicken and vegetables. Bake, uncovered, at 400° for 40 minutes or until chicken is cooked through and vegetables are tender, basting occasionally with juices in pan.

Serves 4

Chicken Parmesan

1 pound skinless and boneless chicken breast tenderloins

⅓ cup grated Parmesan cheese (such as Frigo)

¼ cup cornstarch (such as Argo)

¼ cup potato starch (such as Bob's Red Mill)

Freshly ground black pepper

1 large egg white, lightly beaten

3 tablespoons olive oil

4 ounces (1 cup) Kraft shredded low-moisture part skim mozzarella cheese

16 ounces Tinkyada Brown Rice Pasta, spaghetti style, prepared as directed

26 ounces Prego Traditional pasta sauce

Preheat oven to 350°. Combine cornstarch, potato starch, Parmesan cheese, and pepper in a shallow dish. Dip each chicken tender in egg white. Dredge in cornstarch mixture. Heat oil in a large skillet over medium heat. Add chicken; cook 5 minutes on each side or until golden.

Spread spaghetti in bottom of a 13 x 9-inch baking dish. Arrange chicken over spaghetti and pour the pasta sauce over the chicken. Sprinkle with mozzarella cheese. Bake at 350°F for 15 minutes then broil for 3 minutes.

Serves 4

Tinkyada pasta is sold at specialty foods stores, natural foods stores, and some supermarkets. You may also order the pasta from The Really Great Food Company at www.reallygreatfood.com, or call (800) 593-5377.

Chicken San Juan

1   tablespoon olive oil
1½ pounds skinless and boneless
     chicken breast tenderloins, cut into
     ½-inch pieces
1   medium onion, chopped
1   medium red bell pepper, seeded and
     chopped
2   large garlic cloves, minced or
     pressed
1   teaspoon McCormick oregano leaves

1   bay leaf, whole
12   ounces Kitchen Basics chicken stock
10   ounces (or 1½ cups) frozen green
     peas, thawed
½   teaspoon McCormick paprika
2   teaspoons Argo cornstarch
1   teaspoon salt
     Freshly ground black pepper
3   cups cooked rice, for serving

Heat oil over medium-high heat in a large (12-inch) nonstick skillet. Add the chicken and cook, turning frequently, until lightly browned, about 5 minutes. Add the onion, red pepper, garlic, oregano, and bay leaf. Cover and cook until the vegetables soften, about 4 minutes. Stir in the chicken stock, peas, and paprika and simmer, uncovered, for 2 minutes.

Transfer about 1 tablespoon of the cooking broth into a small bowl. Add the cornstarch and stir until dissolved. Stir the cornstarch mixture into the skillet and cook until the liquid is slightly thickened, about 1 minute. Season with salt and pepper. Discard the bay leaf. Spoon the rice into individual soup bowls and top with the chicken and sauce. Serve immediately.

Serves 4

Chicken with Yellow Peppers and Tomatoes

1½ pounds boneless, skinless chicken breasts
1 tablespoon olive oil
Salt and freshly ground black pepper
⅔ cup dry white wine
½ cup thinly sliced onion
1 yellow bell pepper, chopped

1 medium carrot, sliced thin
1 celery rib, finely chopped
1 clove garlic, minced
1 (14 ounce) can Del Monte diced tomatoes, with their juice
3 cups steamed rice for serving

Wash the chicken pieces in cold running water and pat dry with paper towels. In a large, heavy skillet, heat the oil over moderately high heat. Brown the chicken pieces in the skillet until golden brown on all sides.

Transfer chicken to a platter and season with salt and pepper. Add the wine and boil rapidly until it is reduced by half. Scrape up and loosen any cooking residue in the pan. Lower the heat to medium, add the sliced onion, and cook for about 5 minutes, stirring occasionally. Add the bell pepper, carrot, celery, garlic, and the tomatoes with their juice. Reduce heat to low, cover, and simmer 10 minutes. Add the chicken and cook until tender, about 15 minutes. Turn and baste the chicken a few times while cooking. Serve chicken and sauce over rice.

Serves 4

Garlic Chicken with Roasted Peppers

1½ pounds skinless and boneless
    chicken breasts
20 medium garlic cloves
1½ tablespoons extra virgin olive oil
1   medium green bell pepper
1   medium red bell pepper
1   tablespoon butter

1   large shallot, chopped
4   medium garlic cloves, chopped
¾ cup Chardonnay
¼ cup fresh lemon juice
    (about 2 lemons)
3   cups cooked rice, for serving
    Salt and freshly ground black pepper

Preheat oven to 350°. Toss garlic cloves with 1 tablespoon oil in small glass baking dish. Roast uncovered until garlic is tender and golden, about 30 minutes. Cool 5 minutes. Peel garlic. Set aside.

Arrange peppers on rack of a broiler pan and broil about 2 inches from heat. Rotate peppers on pan as each side blackens, 12 to 15 minutes. Enclose peppers in a paper bag and let stand 10 minutes. Seed peppers, peel, and cut into thin strips.

Melt butter in heavy medium saucepan over low heat. Add shallots and chopped garlic and cook, stirring frequently, 1 minute. Add wine and lemon juice and simmer until reduced to ½ cup, about 7 minutes. Mix in roasted garlic and bell peppers.

Meanwhile, preheat broiler. Brush chicken with remaining oil. Season with salt and pepper. Broil until cooked through, about 5 minutes per side. Place rice and 1 chicken breast on each plate. Spoon sauce over.

Serves 4

Lemon Chicken with Bell Peppers

3 pounds skinless chicken thighs
1 teaspoon McCormick oregano
¼ teaspoon McCormick paprika
½ teaspoon salt
   Freshly ground black pepper
2 teaspoons extra light olive oil

1 medium red bell pepper, cut in strips
1 medium green bell pepper, cut in strips
1 tablespoon freshly grated lemon peel
¼ cup fresh lemon juice

Sprinkle the chicken with oregano, paprika, salt, and pepper. Heat olive oil in a large nonstick skillet over medium-high heat. Add chicken and cook 2 to 3 minutes, turning to brown evenly. Top chicken with bell peppers, lemon peel, and lemon juice. Reduce heat to low and simmer, covered, for 30 minutes, or until chicken is cooked through. Serve with rice.

Serves 4

Ginger Chicken

⅓ cup San-J Tamari wheat free soy sauce

¼ cup orange juice (such as Tropicana Pure Premium)

3 tablespoons finely chopped green onions

1 tablespoon finely chopped peeled fresh ginger

1 tablespoon lemon juice

1 teaspoon McCormick basil leaves

Freshly ground black pepper

⅛ teaspoon McCormick crushed red pepper

¼ teaspoon McCormick allspice

4 garlic cloves, minced

1 pound boneless, skinless chicken breasts, cut into ½-inch-wide strips

2 teaspoons vegetable oil

3 cups hot cooked rice, for serving

Combine soy sauce, orange juice, green onions, ginger, lemon juice, basil, pepper, crushed red pepper, allspice, and garlic in a medium bowl; stir well. Place chicken in a Ziploc bag and add marinade. Marinate in refrigerator 30 minutes. Heat oil in a large nonstick skillet over medium heat. Add chicken, cook and stir, 5 minutes. Cover, reduce heat, and simmer 5 minutes. Serve over rice.

Serves 4

Risotto with Chicken and Mushrooms

4   tablespoons olive oil
8   ounces mushrooms, quartered
½   cup chopped onion
2   cloves garlic, minced
1½ cups Arborio rice
½   cup dry white wine
¼   teaspoon McCormick red pepper
    flakes
30 ounces Kitchen Basics chicken
    stock, heated

2   cups chopped cooked chicken
1   dash (less than ⅛ teaspoon)
    McCormick ground nutmeg
1   tablespoon butter
⅓   cup chopped fresh parsley
¼   cup grated Parmesan cheese
    (such as Frigo), plus more for
    serving
    Freshly ground black pepper

Heat 2 tablespoons oil in a heavy, medium saucepan over medium heat. Add mushrooms and season with pepper. Cook and stir until light brown, about 7 minutes. Transfer mushrooms and any liquid in pan to a bowl.

Add remaining 2 tablespoons oil to pan and heat over low heat. Add onion; cook and stir 5 to 10 minutes or until onion is tender, but not brown. Add garlic and rice and stir until coated. Add wine and stir. Simmer over medium heat 1 to 2 minutes until wine evaporates. Add red pepper flakes and 2 cups hot chicken stock and stir.

Simmer uncovered, stirring occasionally, 9 to 10 minutes or until liquid is absorbed. Add remaining chicken stock and cook, stirring occasionally, 5 minutes. Add chicken and mushrooms and simmer 3 minutes or until rice is al dente and chicken is hot. Remove from heat. Season with nutmeg. Let stand 2 or 3 minutes. Add butter, parsley, and Parmesan cheese. Serve in deep dishes, with more Parmesan.

Serves 6

Rosemary Chicken with Marinara Sauce

4   large boneless skinless chicken
    breast halves (1½ pounds)
1   rosemary sprig
2   tablespoons extra virgin olive oil
1   medium onion, sliced vertically
4   cloves garlic, minced or pressed

Salt and freshly ground black pepper
⅔   cup Newman's Own marinara pasta
    sauce
½   cup Kitchen Basics chicken stock
3   rosemary sprigs, for garnish

Preheat the oven to 375°. Rinse the chicken breasts and pat dry. Arrange chicken in a shallow baking dish to fit. Add rosemary, tucking it under the chicken.

In a nonstick skillet, heat the olive oil over low heat. Add the onion and cook, stirring occasionally, 5 minutes. Add the garlic and cook, stirring, 5 minutes longer. Cover the chicken with the onion mixture. Season with salt and pepper. Top with marinara sauce.

Pour the chicken stock into the bottom of the baking dish and bake until the chicken is cooked through, about 45 to 60 minutes, basting often. Serve the chicken on a platter and spoon the sauce over the top. Garnish with whole rosemary sprigs.

Serves 4

Spanish Rice with Chicken

1   tablespoon vegetable oil
1   pound skinless and boneless chicken breast tenderloins, cut in ½-inch pieces
1   large clove garlic, minced
1   medium onion, chopped
1   medium yellow bell pepper, chopped
½   teaspoon McCormick oregano leaves
1   (14½-ounce) can Del Monte diced tomatoes
3   cups cooked rice, for serving

Heat oil in a large, deep skillet over medium heat. Cook chicken over medium heat for about 4 minutes, turning to brown evenly. Add garlic, onion, bell pepper, and oregano. Cook and stir 3 minutes or until vegetables are crisp-tender. Add tomatoes. Cover, reduce heat to low and simmer 15 minutes. Add rice. Stir to combine ingredients and heat for 2 minutes.

Serves 6

BBQ Chicken

½ cup barbecue sauce (such as Sweet   4   boneless skinless chicken breast
   Baby Ray's)   halves (1½ pounds total)

Place chicken on grill rack over medium-hot heat. Cook 8 minutes; turn chicken and brush with barbecue sauce. Cook an additional 8 minutes or until chicken is cooked through.

Serves 4

Chicken Fajitas

3   tablespoons vegetable oil

1½   pounds skinless and boneless
     chicken breast tenderloins, cut into
     ½-inch pieces

1   large sweet onion, thinly sliced

2   cloves garlic, minced

1   red bell pepper, cut into ½-inch
     strips

½   teaspoon McCormick Hot Mexican
     Style Chili Powder

3   tablespoons fresh lime juice
     (about 2 limes)

10   (6-inch) Mission corn tortillas

1   cup Breakstone's sour cream, for
     accompaniment

1   cup Green Mountain Gringo salsa,
     for accompaniment

1   medium chopped avocado, for
     accompaniment

3   cups cooked rice for serving

Heat 2 tablespoons oil in a large skillet over medium-high heat. Add the chicken; cook and stir until chicken is cooked through, about 5 minutes. Transfer chicken to a platter and set aside.

Heat remaining 1 tablespoon oil in pan. Add onion, garlic, bell pepper, and chili powder. Cook, stirring frequently, until the onion is soft and translucent, about 10 minutes. Add lime juice and reserved chicken to skillet and reheat for about 1 minute. Transfer to a serving platter.

Heat tortillas on griddle over medium-high heat for 10 to 15 seconds on first side, flip and heat 5 to 10 seconds on second side. Serve immediately with small bowls of sour cream, salsa, and avocado on the side.

Serves 4

Chicken Curry

2 tablespoons vegetable oil	3 tablespoons San-J Tamari wheat free soy sauce
1 medium onion, finely chopped	
1⅓ pounds boneless, skinless chicken breasts, cut into 1-inch cubes	3 medium red potatoes, peeled and cubed
1 tablespoon McCormick curry powder	4 medium carrots, chopped ¼-inch thick
1½ cups water	3 cups steamed rice, for serving

In a wok or deep skillet, heat oil over medium-high heat. Add onion and stir-fry until the onion has softened, about 2 minutes. Add the chicken pieces and stir-fry until the chicken is white and firm and no trace of pink remains, 4 to 5 minutes. Stir in curry powder, then water, soy sauce, potatoes, and carrots. Reduce heat to medium, cover and simmer for 10 minutes. Uncover and simmer 10 minutes more or until chicken and vegetables are tender. Serve over rice.

Serves 4

Chicken Fried Rice

3 tablespoons San-J Tamari wheat free soy sauce

2 tablespoons Holland House sherry cooking wine

6 medium sliced green onions, including green tops

2 tablespoons plus 2 teaspoons extra light olive oil, divided

2 large eggs, whisked

1 pound skinless and boneless chicken breast tenderloins, cut into ½-inch pieces

1 tablespoon finely chopped peeled fresh ginger

½ cup Planters dry roasted peanuts, unsalted

1 clove garlic, minced

1 cup chopped onion

8 ounces fresh mushrooms, sliced

2 medium carrots, chopped

1 small zucchini, quartered and sliced thin

¾ pound fresh snow pea pods, whole

1 cup frozen green peas, thawed

4 cups cooked long-grain rice

In a small bowl, combine soy sauce, sherry, and green onions. Set aside.

In a wok, heat 2 teaspoons oil over medium heat, swirling to coat the bottom and sides. Add eggs; cook 1½ minutes or until set, stirring constantly. Remove egg from wok; set aside.

Increase heat to medium-high and heat 1 tablespoon oil. Add chicken; stir and toss 3 minutes. Remove chicken from wok. Set aside and keep warm.

Heat remaining 1 tablespoon oil over medium-high heat. Add ginger, peanuts, and garlic; stir and toss 5 seconds. Add onion, mushrooms, carrots, zucchini, snow pea pods, and peas; stir and toss 3 minutes.

Add soy sauce mixture and stir to combine ingredients. Return egg and chicken to wok. Fluff rice and add to wok; stir to combine and cook an additional 2 minutes.

Serves 6

Advance preparation is very important in stir-frying.
You must chop all of the ingredients and have them lined up in an
area near the wok before you begin stir-frying. Combine any sauces
and don't forget to start the rice in the rice cooker!

Chicken with Tangerine Sauce

2 tablespoons San-J Tamari wheat free soy sauce

2 tablespoons Holland House sherry cooking wine

Finely grated peel of 1 tangerine

1½ pounds skinless and boneless chicken breast tenderloins, cut in ½-inch pieces

⅔ cup tangerine juice (from 2 tangerines)

2 tablespoons Nakano rice vinegar

1 tablespoon cornstarch (such as Argo)

2 tablespoons light olive oil

1 tablespoon finely chopped peeled fresh ginger

3 cloves garlic

¼ teaspoon McCormick crushed red pepper

1 medium red bell pepper, chopped

1 cup sugar snap peas, trimmed

5 green onions, thinly sliced

3 cups hot cooked rice, for serving

To make the marinade, combine the soy sauce, sherry cooking wine and tangerine peel in a small bowl. Stir marinade and pour over chicken. Chill 15 to 30 minutes.

To make the sauce, combine the tangerine juice, vinegar, and cornstarch in glass measuring cup. Whisk to dissolve the cornstarch. Set aside.

In a wok or nonstick skillet, heat 1 tablespoon oil over medium-high heat. Add garlic, ginger, and crushed red pepper. Stir fry about 15 seconds. Add chicken mixture and stir fry until cooked through, about 4 to 5 minutes. Transfer chicken to a shallow bowl.

Add another 1 tablespoon oil to the wok, swirling to coat the bottom and sides. When the oil is hot, add the bell pepper, peas, and green onion. Stir and toss frequently until they begin to soften, about 2 minutes. Return chicken to the wok. Quickly stir the reserved sauce and add it to the wok. Stir and toss over medium-high heat, until the sauce begins to thicken, about 1 minute. Serve immediately over rice.

Serves 4

Kung Pao Chicken

Chicken:

1½ pounds boneless, skinless chicken
    breasts

1 tablespoon cornstarch
    (such as Argo)

1 tablespoon San-J Tamari wheat free
    soy sauce

Trim fat from chicken and cut into 1-inch cubes. Combine cornstarch and soy sauce in a small bowl; stir well and pour over chicken. Cover and chill in refrigerator 15 minutes.

Sherry Mixture:

1 teaspoon cornstarch (such as Argo)

3 tablespoons water

1 tablespoon sugar

3 tablespoons San-J Tamari wheat
    free soy sauce

2 tablespoons Holland House sherry
    cooking wine

1 tablespoon Nakano rice vinegar

In a small bowl, combine cornstarch with 1 tablespoon water. Whisk until cornstarch is dissolved. Add remaining 2 tablespoons water, sugar, soy sauce, sherry cooking wine, and rice vinegar. Stir until well blended. Set aside.

Remaining Ingredients:

2 tablespoons extra light olive oil,
    divided

½ cup Planters dry roasted peanuts,
    unsalted

¼ teaspoon McCormick crushed red
    pepper

4 medium carrots, chopped

1 medium onion, sliced vertically

1 large red bell pepper, chopped

1 tablespoon finely chopped peeled
    fresh ginger

3 cups cooked rice, for serving

Heat 1 teaspoon olive oil in a wok or large nonstick skillet over high heat. Add peanuts and crushed red pepper; stir-fry 30 seconds or until peanuts are golden brown. Remove from pan with a slotted spoon; set aside.

Add remaining 1 tablespoon oil and chicken mixture to pan; stir-fry 4 to 5 minutes. Add carrots, onion, bell pepper, and ginger; stir-fry 1 minute. Add sherry mixture; stir-fry 1 minute or until thick and bubbly. Reduce heat to medium, cover, and steam until carrots are crisp-tender, about 3 minutes. Remove from heat and stir in peanuts.

Serves 4

Quick Chicken Stir-Fry

1   tablespoon olive oil
1   medium onion, cut into wedges
1   medium red bell pepper, cut into
    1-inch pieces
1   small zucchini, sliced
1   clove garlic, minced

2   cups cooked chicken breast, chopped
3   tablespoons balsamic vinegar
3   tablespoons orange juice
2   tablespoons water
    Salt and freshly ground black pepper
3   cups cooked rice, for serving

In a large nonstick skillet, heat oil over medium-high heat. Add onion, red bell pepper, and zucchini. Stir-fry until vegetables are tender, about 5 minutes. Add garlic and cook, stirring constantly, 30 seconds. Stir in chicken, vinegar, orange juice, and water. Season with salt and pepper. Cook until heated through, about 2 minutes.

Serves 4

Stir-Fried Chicken with Peppers and Broccoli

Sauce:

1½ tablespoons San-J Tamari wheat free soy sauce

1½ teaspoons sugar

2 teaspoons Nakano rice vinegar

1 teaspoon cornstarch

1½ tablespoons water

In a small bowl, combine soy sauce, sugar, rice vinegar, cornstarch, and water. Set aside.

Chicken:

3 cups broccoli florets

1½ pounds chicken breast tenderloins, cut into 1-inch pieces

3 tablespoons extra light olive oil

1 medium sweet onion, halved and sliced thin

1 medium yellow bell pepper, cut in ½-inch strips

2 medium garlic cloves, minced or pressed

1 tablespoon finely chopped peeled fresh ginger

⅛ teaspoon McCormick crushed red pepper

3 cups cooked rice, for serving

In a medium saucepan, add broccoli to boiling water and boil 2 minutes. Rinse with cold water and drain.

Heat 2 tablespoons oil in wok over medium-high heat. Add onion and yellow pepper, and stir and toss until softened, about 5 minutes. Remove from pan.

Heat remaining 1 tablespoon oil and stir in garlic, ginger, and crushed red pepper. Add chicken and stir and toss 5 minutes or until cooked through (cut a piece to check). Stir sauce mixture and add to skillet. Add all vegetables and stir and toss until sauce is thickened, about 2 minutes. Serve over rice.

Serves 4

Go to www.nakanovinegar.com to confirm
gluten free status and store locations for rice vinegar.

Stir-Fried Chicken with Broccoli and Mushrooms

1   pound boneless, skinless chicken
    breasts, cut into 1-inch cubes
1   tablespoon cornstarch
1   tablespoon Holland House sherry
    cooking wine
2   tablespoons water
1   tablespoon finely chopped peeled
    fresh ginger

4   tablespoons oil, divided
3   cups broccoli florets
6   ounces mushrooms, sliced
½   cup Kitchen Basics chicken stock
8   ounces sliced water chestnuts,
    canned
3   cups cooked rice, for serving

Combine cornstarch, sherry, and water. Add ginger and stir. Pour sauce over chicken and toss to coat. Let stand 15 minutes.

Heat 2 tablespoons oil in wok over high heat. Add chicken and stir-fry until chicken is no longer pink, about 3 minutes. Remove chicken from pan.

Heat remaining 2 tablespoons oil. Add broccoli and mushrooms and stir-fry to coat with oil, about 2 minutes. Stir in chicken stock and water chestnuts; reduce heat to medium. Simmer, covered, about 2 minutes. Return chicken to pan, and stir to reheat and blend flavors, about 2 minutes. Serve over rice.

Serves 4

Poached Chicken

1 medium onion, sliced
2 carrots, sliced
2 bay leaves
½ teaspoon McCormick thyme leaves

Salt and freshly ground black pepper
3-4 cups water
1½ pounds boneless chicken breasts

In a Dutch oven, combine onion, carrots, bay leaves, thyme, salt, pepper, and water. Bring to a boil. Add chicken and more water if needed to cover chicken. Reduce heat and cover. Simmer over low heat until chicken is tender, about 15 to 20 minutes. Cool 5 minutes; remove skin.

Serves 4

If you are making an entrée or salad recipe that calls for
cooked chicken, try this recipe. It makes 2½ to 3 cups chopped chicken.

Turkey à la King

2 tablespoons unsalted butter

1 tablespoon Bob's Red Mill potato starch

3 celery ribs, chopped

1 medium onion, chopped

¾ cup Kitchen Basics chicken stock

½ cup whole milk

¾ cup frozen peas, thawed in a sieve under warm running water

8 drops Frank's Red Hot cayenne pepper sauce

2 cups cooked turkey or chicken, cut into large chunks

3 cups cooked rice for serving

Place butter in a 4-cup glass measure. Microwave, uncovered, on High (100% power) for 1 minute. Remove from microwave oven and whisk in potato starch. Add celery and onions and cook, uncovered, on High (100% power) for 3 minutes. Remove from microwave oven.

Add ½ cup chicken stock and stir until smooth. Stir in remaining ¼ cup broth and milk. Stir in peas. Cook, uncovered, on High (100% power) for 6 minutes. Remove from microwave oven. Add turkey. Stir and cook, uncovered, on High (100% power) for 2 minutes. Add hot pepper sauce and serve over rice.

Serves 4

A wonderful dish for leftover turkey or chicken.

Grilled Turkey Breast with Marmalade Glaze

1½ pounds Butterball Fresh Turkey Breast for London Broil

2 tablespoons olive oil

¼ cup orange marmalade

¼ cup orange juice (such as Tropicana Pure Premium)

3 cloves garlic, minced or pressed

½ teaspoon McCormick ground ginger

Whisk orange marmalade, orange juice, and ginger in a small bowl. Refrigerate until needed. Combine olive oil and garlic and rub over turkey breast to coat. Grill over medium heat for 1 to 1¼ hours or until thermometer reads 170°. Brush with glaze during the last 15 minutes of cooking. Carve in thin slices diagonally.

Serves 4

Please call Butterball at (800) 288-8372 to confirm gluten-free status of turkey.

Pulled Pork

1 (3-pound) prime pork loin roast
  Salt and freshly ground black pepper
1 tablespoon extra light olive oil
2 medium onions, cut into wedges

8 ounces IBC root beer
6 cloves garlic, minced or pressed
16 ounces prepared barbecue sauce
  (such as Bone Suckin' Sauce)

Preheat oven to 300°. Season the roast with salt and pepper. Heat oil in a Dutch oven over medium heat. Add meat and brown on all sides. Reduce heat to low and drain off fat. Add onions, root beer, and garlic. Cover and cook in oven for 3 hours. Transfer roast to a cutting board or serving platter. Trim fat from meat. Using 2 forks, pull meat apart into shreds. In a large mixing bowl, combine shredded pork and prepared barbecue sauce.

Serves 8

Please call Mott's Inc. at (800) 426-4891 to
confirm the gluten-free status of IBC Root Beer.

Baby Back Ribs

3 pounds pork loin back ribs
   Salt and freshly ground black pepper
1 tablespoon vegetable oil
1 small sweet onion, chopped

1½ cups Sweet Baby Ray's barbecue
   sauce
1½ teaspoons McCormick ground
   mustard
⅓ cup Dole crushed pineapple in juice

Preheat gas grill on high. Reduce heat to medium. Season ribs with pepper and salt and place, bone side down, in center of grill. Grill for 1 to 1½ hours until an instant-read thermometer inserted in the thickest portion of the ribs registers 160°.

For sauce, heat oil in saucepan over medium heat. Add onion and cook and stir for 5 minutes or until tender. Stir in barbecue sauce, mustard, and pineapple. Bring to a boil over medium heat. Reduce heat to low and simmer the sauce, uncovered, about 5 minutes, stirring occasionally. Reserve ½ cup sauce. Brush ribs with sauce during last 10 minutes of grilling. To serve, cut ribs into 4 portions. Spoon reserved sauce over ribs.

Serves 4

Spicy Grilled Pork Chops

1	teaspoon McCormick chili powder	2	garlic cloves, minced or pressed
¾	teaspoon McCormick cumin	4	(½-pound) center-cut boneless pork loin chops
1	teaspoon kosher salt		Freshly ground black pepper
1	tablespoon extra virgin olive oil		

Preheat grill. In a small bowl, mix the chili powder with the cumin and salt. Set aside. In a separate bowl, combine oil and garlic; drizzle over pork chops. Rub spice mixture over the pork chops. Season with black pepper. Grill pork chops 4 minutes over medium-high heat. Turn and cook over medium heat for about 15 minutes, until pork chops are cooked through.

Serves 4

Spicy Grilled Pork Tenderloin

2   pork tenderloins (1 pound each)

¼   cup San-J Tamari wheat free soy sauce

3   tablespoons Domino brown sugar

¾   teaspoon McCormick ground cumin

1   teaspoon McCormick ground mustard

½   teaspoon McCormick paprika

2   large garlic cloves, minced or pressed

2   tablespoons fresh cilantro or parsley (or 1 tablespoon dried)

Combine soy sauce, brown sugar, cumin, mustard, paprika, garlic, and parsley in a 4 cup glass measuring cup. Place tenderloins in a 1 gallon Ziploc bag, add the marinade to bag, push out all air, and seal. Refrigerate for at least 60 minutes. Grill over medium heat for about 12 to 15 minutes on each side - turning once. Slice thinly.

Serves 4

Curried Pork

2 tablespoons extra light olive oil
1 medium onion, finely chopped
1 yellow bell pepper, chopped
1 tablespoon butter
8 ounces fresh mushrooms, sliced
    (about 1½ cups)
2 tablespoons cornstarch (such as Argo)

2 tablespoons potato starch
    (such as Bob's Red Mill)
1 teaspoon McCormick curry powder
1½ pounds boneless pork loin, cut into
    ½-inch pieces
    Freshly ground black pepper
    McCormick sea salt
1 (14½-ounce) can Del Monte diced
    tomatoes, undrained

Preheat oven to 350°. Lightly grease an 11 x 7-inch covered baking dish. Heat 1 tablespoon olive oil in a large nonstick skillet over medium-high heat. Add onion and bell pepper, cook and stir 8 minutes. Add butter and mushrooms. Cook and stir, 2 minutes. Cool slightly and spread into prepared baking dish.

Combine cornstarch, potato starch, and curry powder in a medium bowl. Add pork, toss to coat and season with pepper and salt. Heat 1 tablespoon olive oil in skillet over medium-high heat. Add pork mixture and brown on all sides, about 5 minutes. Spread pork mixture over onion mixture. Pour tomatoes over pork mixture and spread evenly. Cover and bake at 350° for 1 hour.

Serves 4

Kung Pao Pork

Sauce:

1	tablespoon sugar
3	tablespoons water
3	tablespoons San-J Tamari wheat free soy sauce
2	tablespoons Holland House sherry cooking wine

1	tablespoon Heinz distilled white vinegar
1	teaspoon cornstarch (such as Argo)
1½	teaspoons Stonewall Kitchen toasted sesame oil
¼	teaspoon salt

Combine sugar, water, soy sauce, sherry, vinegar, cornstarch, sesame oil, and salt in a small bowl; stir until well-blended. Set aside.

Pork:

1	pound pork tenderloin
1	tablespoon cornstarch
1	tablespoon San-J Tamari wheat free soy sauce
1	tablespoon vegetable oil, divided
¼	teaspoon McCormick crushed red pepper

1	large red bell pepper, coarsely chopped
¾	cup onion, sliced vertically
1	tablespoon finely chopped peeled fresh ginger
½	cup Planters dry-roasted peanuts, unsalted
3	cups cooked rice, for serving

Cut pork into 1-inch cubes. Combine pork, 1 tablespoon cornstarch, and 1 tablespoon soy sauce in a bowl; stir well. Cover and marinate in refrigerator 15 minutes.

Heat 1 teaspoon vegetable oil in a wok or large nonstick skillet over high heat. Add peanuts and crushed red pepper; stir-fry 30 seconds or until peanuts are golden brown. Add remaining oil and pork mixture to pan; stir-fry 2 minutes. Add bell pepper, onion, and ginger; stir-fry 1 minute or until vegetables are crisp-tender. Add sauce mixture; stir-fry 1 minute or until thick and bubbly.

Serves 4

Please go to the Consumer FAQs at heinz.com to
confirm the gluten-free status of Heinz Distilled White Vinegar.

Sweet and Sour Pork

1   (8-ounce) can Dole pineapple tidbits in juice

2   tablespoons cornstarch (such as Argo)

¼   cup Domino® light brown sugar

¼   cup Heinz distilled white vinegar

2   tablespoons San-J Tamari wheat free soy sauce

¼   teaspoon McCormick crushed red pepper

1   tablespoon extra light olive oil

1   pound lean boneless pork, cut into 1-inch cubes

½   cup chopped onion

1   medium red bell pepper, cut into strips

1   medium green bell pepper, coarsely chopped

1   cup sliced zucchini

3   cups hot cooked rice, for serving

Drain pineapple. Reserve juice. Add cornstarch to reserved juice; whisk to combine. Add brown sugar, vinegar, soy sauce, and crushed red pepper. Stir well and set aside.

Heat oil in a wok or large nonstick skillet over medium-high heat. Add pork; cook 3 minutes or until pork loses its pink color. Add onion; stir-fry 1 minute. Add bell peppers and zucchini; stir-fry 4 minutes or until crisp-tender. Stir in pineapple and pineapple juice mixture. Cook 30 seconds or until thickened, stirring constantly. Serve over rice.

Serves 4

Please go to the Consumer FAQs at heinz.com to confirm the gluten-free status of Heinz Distilled White Vinegar.

Grilled Halibut with Lemon Sauce

⅜ cup Kitchen Basics chicken stock
2 tablespoons fresh lemon juice
1½ teaspoons cornstarch
½ tablespoon minced fresh parsley
¼ teaspoon salt
⅛ teaspoon McCormick oregano leaves

⅛ teaspoon McCormick rosemary leaves, crushed
4 (6-ounce) halibut fillets
Vegetable cooking spray, to coat grill rack

Combine chicken stock, lemon juice, and cornstarch in a small saucepan; stir well. Bring to a boil and cook 1 minute, stirring constantly. Remove from heat. Stir in parsley, salt, oregano, and rosemary. Cover and set aside.

Place fillets on grill rack coated with cooking spray; grill, covered, 6 minutes on each side or until the fish flakes easily when tested with a fork. Serve with sauce.

Serves 4

Grilled Salmon with Orange Sauce

1½ pounds boneless, skinless salmon fillet, cut in 4 pieces

½ cup Smucker's orange marmalade

1 teaspoon finely chopped peeled fresh ginger

1 clove garlic, minced or pressed

2 tablespoons rice vinegar (such as Nakano)

2 teaspoons San-J Tamari wheat free soy sauce

3 green onions, thinly sliced

In a small bowl, combine marmalade, ginger, garlic, vinegar, soy sauce, and green onions. Place marinade in one-gallon Ziploc bag. Add fish and marinate for 10 minutes while pre-heating grill. Place salmon on a grill rack coated with cooking spray. Grill over medium heat, covered, 5 to 6 minutes on each side.

Serves 4

Go to www.nakanovinegar.com for
gluten-free status and store locations for Nakano rice vinegar.

Grilled Tuna

1¼ pounds tuna steaks
1   tablespoon lime juice
1   tablespoon extra light olive oil

3   large garlic cloves, minced or pressed
Salt and freshly ground black pepper

Combine lime juice and olive oil in a small bowl. Whisk to combine. Add garlic, salt, and pepper. Place tuna steaks in a one gallon Ziploc bag. Pour in marinade and refrigerate for 15 minutes. Remove tuna from marinade and grill over medium heat for 5 minutes. Turn and grill for approximately 4 more minutes.

Serves 4

Tuna and Red Pepper Skewers

1   pound tuna fillets, cut into 1-inch cubes

½   cup lime juice (from 2 limes)

3   tablespoons extra light olive oil

2   tablespoons sugar

½   teaspoon McCormick chili powder

1   large red bell pepper, cut into 1-inch pieces

6   medium green onions, cut into 1-inch pieces

Salt and freshly ground black pepper

Whisk lime juice, oil, sugar, and chili powder in a small bowl. Transfer half of the sauce to a serving dish and let stand at room temperature. Arrange tuna pieces, red bell pepper, and onion pieces on 4 skewers. Place skewers in a large, shallow container and season with salt and pepper. Brush remaining sauce over kabobs. Let fish marinate in sauce for 15 minutes. Grill tuna over medium heat, turning occasionally, about 12 minutes. Serve kabobs with sauce.

Serves 4

Dakota Lakes Tilapia

4 (4-ounce) tilapia fillets	¼ cup water
¼ cup Dakota Lakes Gourmet Coating	3 tablespoons extra light olive oil

Spread Dakota Lakes Gourmet Coating in a shallow bowl. Dip fillets in water, then in Dakota Lakes Gourmet Coating, turning to coat completely. Heat oil in a nonstick skillet over medium heat. Add fillets and cook about 3 to 5 minutes on each side.

Serves 4

Dakota Lakes Gourmet Coating is available
at the Gluten-Free Pantry (www.glutenfreepantry.com).

Orange and Ginger Salmon

4 (6-ounce) salmon fillets (1-inch thick), skinned

1 cup orange juice

1 tablespoon San-J Tamari wheat free soy sauce

2 teaspoons finely chopped peeled fresh ginger

1 teaspoon Maille Dijon style mustard

1 tablespoon extra light olive oil

To make marinade, combine orange juice, soy sauce, ginger, and mustard in a small bowl. Place fish in a shallow baking dish. Pour ½ of the marinade over the fish. Cover and refrigerate 45 minutes.

Heat oil in a nonstick skillet over medium heat. Cook salmon, covered, 7 minutes. Turn salmon over; add reserved marinade. Cover, and cook until salmon is cooked through, about 4 minutes.

Serves 4

Salmon with Ginger and Curry

1 tablespoon finely chopped peeled fresh ginger

2 teaspoons McCormick curry powder

Salt and freshly ground black pepper

4 (6-ounce) salmon fillets (about 1-inch thick), skinned

1 tablespoon extra light olive oil

3 green onions, chopped

In a small bowl, combine ginger, curry, salt, and pepper. Rub spice mixture onto both sides of salmon fillets. Heat oil in a large, nonstick skillet over medium heat. Cook salmon 7 minutes. Turn salmon over and cook, covered, until cooked through, about 4 minutes. Add green onions and cook 30 seconds.

Serves 4

Tomato Salsa Orange Roughy

1   pound orange roughy fillets

⅓   cup Green Mountain Gringo salsa

½   teaspoon Lea & Perrins
     Worcestershire sauce

½   teaspoon extra light olive oil

    Salt and freshly ground black pepper

In a small bowl, combine salsa, Worcestershire sauce, oil, salt, and pepper. Stir to combine. Place fish in microwave-safe baking dish. Pour salsa mixture over fish. Cover dish with plastic wrap and turn back one corner to vent. Microwave on High (100% power) for 6 minutes or until fish flakes easily when tested with a fork. Let stand 1 to 2 minutes to complete cooking.

Serves 4

Rice with Tuna, Broccoli, and Parmesan

1   red onion, chopped
1   tablespoon butter
1   cup Arborio rice
16 ounces Kitchen Basics chicken stock
¼   cup dry white wine, such as Pinot Grigio or Sauvignon Blanc
    Freshly ground black pepper

8   ounces broccoli slaw (found in produce aisle near bagged salad mixes)
1   can (6 ounces) Bumble Bee albacore tuna in spring water, drained
¾   cup half-and-half
½   cup freshly grated Parmesan cheese (such as Frigo)

Place the onion and butter in a microwave-safe, 2 quart baking dish with a lid. Cover and microwave on high (100% power) for 5 minutes, stirring once. Stir in the rice. Cook, covered, on high (100% power) for 2 minutes. Stir in the chicken stock and wine. Season with pepper. Cook, covered, on high (100% power) for 10 minutes.

Stir in the broccoli slaw; cook, covered, on medium (50% power) power until rice is just tender and slaw is crisp-tender, about 5 minutes. Stir in the half-and-half and tuna. Cook, covered, on medium (50% power) for 30 seconds. Let stand for 3 minutes. Stir in the Parmesan cheese.

Serves 4

Please go to the Consumer FAQs at bumblebee.com to confirm the gluten-free status of Bumble Bee Brand canned seafood products.

Caribbean Shrimp with Rice and Beans

1	tablespoon extra light olive oil	1	cup chopped tomato
¾	pound medium-sized shrimp, peeled and deveined	¼	teaspoon McCormick crushed red pepper
1	medium sweet onion, chopped	¼	teaspoon McCormick ground cumin
½	cup chopped celery	2	cups cooked rice
1	medium yellow bell pepper	1	can Westbrae black beans, drained
3	large garlic cloves, minced or pressed	¼	cup fresh cilantro leaves, chopped

In wok or large nonstick skillet, heat 1 tablespoon olive oil over medium-high heat, swirling to coat the bottom and sides of the pan. Add shrimp and stir-fry until shrimp is pink and firm, about 3 to 4 minutes. Transfer shrimp to a bowl.

Add onion, celery, bell pepper, and garlic. Stir-fry 5 minutes. Add chopped tomato, crushed red pepper, and cumin and stir-fry for 2 minutes. Stir in cooked rice, black beans, cilantro, and shrimp and cook for 1 minute or until heated.

Serves 4

POTATOES, RICE
& VEGETABLES

Potatoes, Rice & Vegetables

Potato Fans

4 medium Yukon Gold potatoes
1 tablespoon olive oil
1 teaspoon coarse salt
1 teaspoon freshly ground black pepper
½ teaspoon McCormick basil leaves

Scrub potatoes and dry well. Cut potatoes into very thin slices (about ⅛-inch thick) almost to but not through the bottom of the potato. Potatoes should remain whole. Place potatoes in an oiled roasting pan and brush with olive oil. Sprinkle with coarse salt, pepper, and basil. Roast potatoes in a preheated 400° oven for 50 to 60 minutes, or until potatoes fan out and become golden brown and crispy. Serve immediately.

Serves 4

Roasted Fingerling Potatoes

1½ pounds French fingerling potatoes   1   tablespoon olive oil
     (or mini red potatoes)   ¼   teaspoon kosher salt

Preheat oven to 425°. Put potatoes in a 8 x 11 glass baking dish. Drizzle potatoes with oil and toss to coat. Sprinkle with salt. Roast potatoes in middle of oven until tender when pierced with a sharp paring knife, about 40 minutes.

Serves 4

Roasted Potatoes

4 medium Yukon Gold potatoes
   (about 1 pound), scrubbed well
   and quartered

1 tablespoon extra virgin olive oil
½ teaspoon kosher salt

Preheat oven to 425°. Stir together oil and salt in small shallow baking dish or pie plate. Add potatoes and rub with oil mixture to coat. Roast potatoes in middle of oven until tender when pierced with a sharp paring knife, about 40 minutes.

Serves 4

Baked Potatoes

4   large baking potatoes

Scrub baking potatoes with a brush or sponge. Prick potatoes 4 times on each side with a fork. Bake in a 425° degree oven for 60 minutes. When done, roll gently under your hand. Cut a crisscross in the top with a knife. Press ends and push up.

Serves 4

Twice Baked Potatoes

4   slices Oscar Mayer bacon
1   tablespoon extra light olive oil
3   garlic cloves, minced
4   medium baking potatoes
    (about 2 pounds)
1   cup Breakstone's sour cream

2   ounces Heluva® Good Cheddar
    cheese, shredded (½ cup), divided
⅓   cup minced green onions, divided
¼   cup milk
¼   teaspoon salt
    Freshly ground black pepper

Preheat oven to 425°. Cook bacon in a nonstick skillet over medium heat until crisp. Remove from skillet; crumble and set aside. Wipe skillet clean with paper towels. Heat oil in skillet over medium heat. Add garlic; cook and stir 1 minute. Set aside.

Bake potatoes at 425° for 1 hour or until done; cool slightly. Cut a lengthwise slit across top of potatoes; carefully scoop pulp into a bowl, leaving shells intact. Add half of crumbled bacon, garlic, sour cream, ¼ cup cheese, 3 tablespoons onions, milk, and salt to pulp; mash.

Increase oven temperature to 450°. Stuff shells with potato mixture; top with remaining crumbled bacon, cheese, and onions. Place the stuffed potatoes on a baking sheet. Bake at 450° for 15 minutes or until potatoes are thoroughly heated. Season with pepper, if desired.

Serves 4

Broccoli Cheddar Twice Baked Potatoes

4   medium baking potatoes
1   cup plain yogurt (such as Dannon)
½   teaspoon salt
⅛   teaspoon McCormick paprika

4   ounces Cheddar cheese (such as
    Heluva® Good), shredded (1 cup)
2   cups broccoli florets
    Freshly ground black pepper

Wash potatoes well. Dry and pierce several times with a fork. Bake at 425° for about 1 hour or until soft. Cool slightly and cut potatoes in half lengthwise. Carefully scoop potato pulp into bowl, leaving a thin layer of pulp to keep skin intact. Set potato skins aside.

To pulp, add yogurt, salt, paprika, and ½ cup of the cheese. Season with pepper. Mix until light and fluffy. Cook broccoli florets in a large pot of boiling salted water until just tender, about 5 minutes. Stir broccoli into potato mixture and stuff potato skins with mixture.

Place on ungreased baking sheet and sprinkle with remaining cheese. Reduce oven temperature to 375° and bake for 15 to 20 minutes or until potato is hot.

Serves 4

Garlic Fries

2	large baking potatoes, cut in ¼-inch strips	1	tablespoon butter
2	teaspoons vegetable oil	4	medium garlic cloves, minced
¼	teaspoon salt	1	teaspoon McCormick parsley
	Cooking spray (such as PAM)	1	tablespoon freshly grated Parmesan cheese (such as Frigo)

Preheat oven to 400°. Combine potatoes, oil, and salt in a large Ziploc bag, tossing to coat. Arrange potatoes in a single layer on a baking sheet coated with cooking spray. Bake at 400° for 50 minutes or until potatoes are tender and golden brown, turning after 20 minutes. Place butter and garlic in a large skillet. Cook over low heat 2 minutes, stirring frequently. Add potatoes, parsley, and cheese to pan; toss to coat. Serve immediately.

Serves 4

Mashed Potatoes with Butter

5   medium red potatoes, whole   ¼   cup milk, heated
2   tablespoons butter

   Peel potatoes and cut into ¼-inch slices. Add potatoes to a 4-quart saucepan and cover
with cold water by 1-inch. Bring water to a boil, then reduce heat and simmer potatoes
until tender, about 20 minutes. Drain. Mash with a potato masher. Add butter and
gradually beat in enough of the hot milk to make light and fluffy.

Serves 4

Garlic Mashed Potatoes

6 medium garlic cloves, unpeeled
2 tablespoons extra light olive oil
3 medium baking potatoes, peeled
   and cut into small chunks

2 tablespoons butter
½ cup whole milk
   Salt and freshly ground black pepper

Preheat oven to 325°. Place garlic cloves in a small ovenproof baking dish. Drizzle with the olive oil. Cover with foil and bake for 35 minutes, until very soft. When cooled, squeeze the garlic from their skins into a small bowl and mash with a fork.

Place potatoes in a saucepan. Cover with water; bring to a boil. Reduce heat. Simmer 20 minutes, or until tender; drain. Return potatoes to pan and add garlic to pan. Add butter and milk and mash with a potato masher. Season with salt and pepper.

Serves 4

Scalloped Potatoes with Boursin

2½ ounces Boursin cheese (half of the 5 ounce package)

2 tablespoons butter

¾ cup whole milk

4 medium Yukon Gold potatoes, scrubbed and thinly sliced

Salt and freshly ground black pepper

Preheat oven to 400°. In a saucepan over medium heat, melt the Boursin cheese and butter with the milk until smooth.

In a 8 x 11 baking dish, arrange half of the sliced potatoes in slightly overlapping rows. Season with salt and pepper. Pour half of the cheese mixture over the potatoes. Arrange remaining potatoes in slightly overlapping rows on top of the potatoes in the dish. Pour remaining cheese mixture over potatoes.

Bake about 1 hour, until top is golden brown and potatoes are tender when pierced with a fork.

Serves 4

Curried Rice

2	cups rice	2	cloves garlic
2	small apples (such as Braeburn), peeled and cored	2	tablespoons McCormick curry powder
3	tablespoons butter	1	medium bay leaf, whole
1	cup onion, finely chopped	3	cups Kitchen Basics chicken stock

Chop the apples into ¼-inch cubes. There should be about 2 cups. Do not use more. Set aside.

Heat the butter in a saucepan and add the onion and garlic. Cook and stir until onion wilts, about 8 minutes. Add the apple and curry powder and stir. Add the rice, bay leaf, and chicken stock.

Bring rice to a boil; reduce heat to low. Cover with a tight fitting lid and cook exactly 17 minutes. Let stand 10 minutes to soften.

Serves 4

Rice with Peas and Onions

1   tablespoon butter
1   medium onion, finely chopped

1   cup Green Giant frozen peas
2   cups cooked rice, kept warm

Melt butter in a saucepan over medium heat and add the onion. Cook, stirring, until wilted, about 2 minutes. Add peas and cook and stir for 1 minute. Add onion and peas to cooked rice. Stir to fluff rice. Let stand, covered, 5 minutes.

Serves 4

Spanish Rice

1   tablespoon extra light olive oil
½   cup chopped onion
2   garlic cloves, minced or pressed
¼   cup chopped green bell pepper
¼   cup chopped red bell pepper
¼   cup Contadina tomato sauce

1   teaspoon McCormick chili powder
¼   teaspoon McCormick crushed red
    pepper
1   (14½-ounce) can Del Monte diced
    tomatoes
3   cups cooked rice

Heat oil in a large nonstick skillet over medium heat. Add onion, garlic, and bell peppers. Cook and stir 2 minutes or until tender. Add tomato sauce, chili powder, crushed red pepper, and tomatoes. Cook 2 minutes, stirring frequently. Reduce heat to low. Add rice and stir and cook until thoroughly heated, about 3 minutes.

Serves 6

Rice and Corn Casserole

1½ cups Lundburg short grain brown rice, prepared as directed

9 ounces frozen Green Giant Niblets Corn (No Sauce), thawed

1 small onion, finely chopped

8 ounces Heluva® Good New York State extra-sharp Cheddar cheese, shredded (2 cups)

1 can (4.5 ounces) Old El Paso Chopped Green Chiles

1 cup milk

½ teaspoon McCormick chili powder
Freshly ground black pepper
McCormick paprika

Preheat oven to 350°. In a large mixing bowl, combine all the ingredients except the paprika, and mix until well blended. Pour mixture into a greased 2-quart baking dish. Sprinkle with paprika. Bake, covered, for 40 minutes.

Serves 6

Wild Rice Casserole

1   cup wild rice
1   cup white rice
1   cup dried currants
½   cup pine nuts
1   tablespoon McCormick parsley
      flakes

2   tablespoons grated orange peel,
      from 2 oranges
¼   cup olive oil
2   tablespoons fresh orange juice
      Salt and freshly ground black pepper
      Freshly grated Parmesan cheese
      (such as Frigo)

Preheat the oven to 350°. Bring 3 cups water to a boil in a medium size heavy saucepan. Add the wild rice, stir and reduce the heat. Cover the pan and simmer the rice for 45 minutes or until tender. Drain the rice, if necessary, and transfer it to a large bowl.

Bring 2 cups of water to a boil in a heavy saucepan. Add the white rice, stir and reduce the heat. Cover the pan, and simmer the rice for 20 minutes. The water should be totally absorbed and the rice just tender. Transfer the white rice to the bowl with the wild rice.

Add the remaining ingredients, except the Parmesan cheese, to the rices, and toss to combine. Transfer the rice mixture to an ovenproof baking dish, cover tightly with aluminum foil, and bake until the rices are soft but not mushy, and the casserole is heated through, 20 to 30 minutes. Sprinkle with Parmesan cheese and serve.

Serves 8

Dried currants are available at www.kingarthurflour.com or call (802) 649-3881.

Wild Rice Pilaf

4 tablespoons unsalted butter
1½ cups wild rice
3 cups Kitchen Basics chicken stock
1 tablespoon fresh lemon juice
   Salt and freshly ground black pepper

⅓ cup pistachio nuts or toasted pine
   nuts
⅔ cup sliced green onions
2 tablespoons finely chopped fresh
   parsley

Melt butter in a heavy saucepan over medium heat. Add wild rice and cook, stirring, until rice is coated with the butter. Pour in chicken broth and bring to a boil. Reduce the heat to low, cover pan, and cook the rice until all liquid is absorbed. This will take approximately 1 hour. Remove from heat, and stir in lemon juice. Season with salt and pepper. Just before serving, fluff rice with a fork and stir in pistachios, green onions, and parsley.

Serves 6

To toast pine nuts, place on a baking sheet
and bake at 350° for 3 to 5 minutes, until lightly browned.

Baked Beans

2   (18 ounce) jars B & M baked beans   ⅓   cup Heinz ketchup
1   small onion, finely chopped   2   teaspoons McCormick ground
⅓   cup firmly packed Domino dark   mustard
    brown sugar

Preheat oven to 350°. In a 2-quart baking dish, stir together baked beans, onion, brown sugar, ketchup, and mustard. Bake, uncovered, 1 hour or until bubbly.

Serves 8

Roasted Carrots

2	tablespoons unsalted butter	2	tablespoons sugar
2	pounds carrots, cut into 1-inch slices	1	teaspoon finely chopped peeled fresh ginger
¼	cup orange juice (such as Tropicana Pure Premium)	¼	teaspoon kosher salt
2	tablespoons fresh lemon juice	⅛	teaspoon McCormick ground cumin

Place rack on second level from the bottom of oven. Heat oven to 450°. Put melted butter and carrot slices in a 14 x 9 x 2 glass baking pan. Toss carrots until slices are lightly coated. Arrange slices in pan in a single layer. Roast 15 minutes.

Meanwhile, in a small bowl, combine orange juice, lemon juice, sugar, ginger, salt, and cumin. Remove pan from oven and pour orange juice mixture over carrots. Using a spatula, turn carrots over in the liquid. Roast 10 minutes more. Carrots should be easy to pierce with a fork, but still firm.

Serves 6

Steamed Carrots

6   whole carrots

Peel and cut carrots into ¼-inch slices. To steam, place 1-inch of water in a medium saucepan. Place a collapsible steaming basket in the pan. Then put the vegetables in the steaming basket and cover tightly. Heat over high heat until water boils. Reduce heat to medium-low, but make sure it is high enough to keep the water bubbling. Steam until crisp-tender, 8 to 10 minutes.

Serves 4

Green Beans with Shallots

1	pound green beans	2	teaspoons water
2	teaspoons olive oil		Salt and freshly ground black pepper
2	tablespoons minced shallots		

Trim ends from beans. Drop beans into a large stockpot of boiling water; cook 10 minutes or until crisp-tender. Drain. Heat oil in stockpot over medium heat. Add shallots; cook and stir 3 minutes or until tender. Add green beans and water; cook 3 minutes or until beans are tender, stirring occasionally. Remove from heat, and season with salt and pepper.

Serves 4

Roasted Peppers with Garlic

2	medium red bell peppers	2	tablespoons extra virgin olive oil
2	medium yellow bell peppers		Salt
1	large garlic clove, thinly sliced		

Preheat broiler. Quarter bell peppers lengthwise and discard stems, seeds and ribs. Arrange peppers, skin sides up, on rack of a broiler pan and broil about 2 inches from heat until skins are blistered, 8 to 12 minutes.

Transfer roasted peppers to a bowl and let stand, covered, until cool enough to handle. Peel peppers and cut each quarter lengthwise into 2 or 3 strips. In a medium bowl, combine peppers, oil, garlic, and salt. Refrigerate peppers, covered, at least 3 hours and up to 3 days.

Serves 6

Spinach with Garlic

1 tablespoon extra light olive oil
1 pound spinach
2 garlic cloves, minced or pressed

Freshly ground black pepper and salt
1 tablespoon freshly grated Parmesan cheese (such as Frigo)

Heat the olive oil in a large skillet over medium-high heat. Add the spinach and stir and toss rapidly for about 1 minute. Cover and cook until wilted, about 2 minutes. Uncover and raise the heat to high to burn away any excess liquid. Add the garlic; cook and stir for 1 minute. Season with freshly ground pepper and salt. Serve immediately with Parmesan cheese.

Serves 4

PASTA & PIZZA

Pasta & Pizza

Baked Pasta

8   ounces (2 cups) Tinkyada elbow or penne pasta
1   pound ground sirloin
26 ounces Prego Traditional pasta sauce

⅓   cup freshly grated Parmesan cheese (such as Stella)
8   ounces (2 cups) Kraft shredded low-moisture part skim mozzarella cheese

Preheat oven to 350°. Cook pasta according to package directions. When pasta is cooked, drain and rinse thoroughly with cold water. Meanwhile cook ground sirloin in a large skillet over medium heat until browned. Drain fat. Add pasta sauce to browned sirloin in skillet and simmer for 10 minutes.

In a 11 x 8-inch baking dish, spread ½ cup meat sauce to cover bottom. Add drained pasta to the remaining meat sauce in the skillet and stir to combine. Spoon ½ of the pasta mixture into the baking dish.

Evenly top with half of the Parmesan cheese. Add the remaining pasta mixture. Sprinkle with remaining Parmesan cheese and top with mozzarella cheese. Bake 25 minutes, covered, until heated through and cheese is melted. Uncover and broil until lightly browned, about 2 minutes.

Serves 6

Tinkyada pasta is sold at specialty foods stores, natural foods stores, and some supermarkets. You may also order the pasta from The Really Great Food Company at www.reallygreatfood.com, or call (800) 593-5377.

Fettuccine with Shrimp and Broccoli

14 ounces Tinkyada fettuccine
¼ cup extra virgin olive oil
3 cloves garlic, minced or pressed
1 medium bunch broccoli, cut into tiny florets

1 pound medium shrimp, peeled and deveined
½ cup dry white wine
Salt and freshly ground black pepper

Prepare the fettuccine according to package directions. Rinse and drain the pasta.

In a large skillet, heat the olive oil over low heat. Add the garlic and cook, stirring frequently, about 2 minutes. Add the broccoli, cover and cook, stirring occasionally, until tender, about 5 minutes. Increase heat to medium, add the shrimp and cook and stir for 2 minutes. Add the wine and season with salt and pepper. Cook for 2 minutes longer. Transfer pasta to the skillet and cook and stir for 2 minutes.

Serves 6

Tinkyada pasta is sold at specialty foods stores, natural foods stores, and some supermarkets. You may also order the pasta from The Really Great Food Company at www.reallygreatfood.com, or call (800) 593-5377.

Spaghetti with Meat Sauce

16 ounces Tinkyada spaghetti
1   pound ground sirloin
26 ounces Prego Traditional pasta
    sauce
1   tablespoon vegetable oil

1   tablespoon butter
1   red bell pepper, chopped
8   ounces mushroom, sliced
    Grated Parmesan cheese (such as
    Frigo), for serving

Cook pasta according to package directions. When pasta is cooked, drain and rinse thoroughly with cold water.

Cook sirloin in a large skillet over medium heat until brown; drain fat. Add pasta sauce to browned sirloin and simmer for 10 minutes. In a medium nonstick skillet, heat oil and butter. Add bell peppers and mushrooms, cook and stir until softened, about 10 minutes. Add vegetables to pasta sauce.

Divide pasta among four plates and top with sauce. Serve with Parmesan cheese.

Serves 4

Please call (888) 367-7734 to obtain a list of gluten-free
Campbell Soup Company products including Prego.

Spaghetti Pizza

12 ounces Tinkyada organic brown rice pasta, spaghetti style
2 eggs
½ cup milk
16 ounces (4 cups) Kraft shredded low-moisture part skim mozzarella cheese
¾ teaspoon McCormick garlic powder
½ teaspoon salt
1 pound ground beef
26 ounces Prego Traditional pasta sauce
¾ teaspoon McCormick oregano
24 slices Hormel pepperoni

Preheat oven to 350°. Grease a 13 x 9-inch baking dish. Break spaghetti into 3-inch pieces. Cook spaghetti according to package directions and drain.

In a large bowl, beat eggs and milk. Add 1 cup mozzarella cheese, garlic powder, and salt. Stir in spaghetti. Spread into prepared baking dish. Bake for 10 minutes.

In a large skillet over medium heat, cook and stir ground beef until brown; drain fat. Spread ground beef over spaghetti. Pour pasta sauce over ground beef. Sprinkle with oregano and remaining 3 cups mozzarella cheese. Arrange pepperoni slices over top. Bake at 350° for an additional 25 to 30 minutes. Let stand 5 minutes. Cut into squares and serve.

Serves 8

Tinkyada pasta is sold at specialty foods stores, natural foods stores, and some supermarkets. You may also order the pasta from The Really Great Food Company at www.reallygreatfood.com, or call (800) 593-5377.

Lasagna

1   pound ground sirloin
26 ounces Prego Traditional pasta sauce
1   cup small curd cottage cheese (such as Breakstone's)

8   ounces (2 cups) Kraft shredded low-moisture part skim mozzarella cheese
⅓   cup freshly grated Parmesan cheese (such as Frigo)
9   **Tinkyada brown rice lasagna noodles (¾ of 10-ounce package)**

Preheat oven to 350°. Cook noodles according to package instructions. Cook meat in large saucepan over medium heat until browned. Drain fat. Add pasta sauce and simmer 5 minutes.

Spread 1 cup meat sauce in bottom of 13 x 9-inch baking dish. Arrange 3 noodles over meat mixture; top with 1 cup meat sauce, ½ cup cottage cheese, 1 cup mozzarella cheese and half of the Parmesan cheese. Repeat with 3 lasagna noodles, spread with 1 cup sauce, ½ cup cottage cheese, and remaining 1 cup mozzarella cheese. Add remaining 3 lasagna noodles, spread with 1 cup sauce and remaining Parmesan cheese.

Cover and bake at 350° for 30 minutes. Let stand 10 minutes before serving.

Serves 6

Tinkyada pasta is sold at specialty foods stores, natural foods stores, and some supermarkets. You may also order the pasta from The Really Great Food Company at www.reallygreatfood.com, or call (800) 593-5377.

Vegetable Lasagna

9   Tinkyada brown rice lasagna
    noodles (¾ of 10 ounce package)
2   red or yellow bell peppers
1   tablespoon olive oil
1   small onion, chopped
4   garlic cloves, minced or pressed
2   cups chopped zucchini
1½ cups sliced mushrooms
½   teaspoon McCormick oregano leaves

    Freshly ground black pepper
26 ounces Prego Traditional pasta
    sauce
1½ cups 2% low-fat cottage cheese
    (such as Breakstone's)
8   ounces (2 cups) Kraft shredded
    low-moisture part skim mozzarella
    cheese
⅓   cup freshly grated Parmesan cheese
    (such as Frigo)

Preheat oven to 350°. Cook noodles according to package instructions.

Arrange peppers on rack of a broiler pan and broil about 2 inches from heat. Rotate peppers on pan as each side blackens, 12 to 15 minutes. Enclose peppers in a paper bag and let stand 10 minutes. Seed peppers, peel and cut into thin strips.

Heat olive oil in a large nonstick skillet. Add onion and garlic. Cook and stir 2 minutes. Add zucchini and mushrooms and cook, stirring occasionally, 3 minutes. Add roasted peppers and oregano. Season with black pepper. Remove from heat and set aside.

Spread 1 cup pasta sauce in bottom of 11 x 7 x 2-inch baking dish. Arrange 3 noodles over pasta sauce; top with half of the vegetable mixture, ¾ cup cottage cheese, 1 cup mozzarella cheese, and half of the Parmesan cheese. Repeat with 1 cup pasta sauce, 3 lasagna noodles, remaining vegetable mixture, ¾ cup cottage cheese, and remaining mozzarella cheese. Add remaining 3 lasagna noodles, spread with 1 cup sauce and remaining Parmesan cheese.

Cover and bake at 350° for 30 minutes. Let stand 10 minutes before serving.

Serves 4

Tinkyada pasta is sold at specialty foods stores, natural foods stores,
and some supermarkets. You may also order the pasta from The Really Great
Food Company at www.reallygreatfood.com, or call (800) 593-5377.

Mushroom and Pepperoni Pizza

1   Gluten-free pizza crust mix (Really Great Food Company or Mona's)
2   tablespoons extra virgin olive oil, divided
2   cloves garlic, minced or pressed
28 ounces Del Monte diced tomatoes, drained
¼   teaspoon McCormick oregano leaves, crushed

½   teaspoon McCormick basil leaves
2   tablespoons Contadina tomato paste
8   ounces (2 cups) Kraft shredded low-moisture part skim mozzarella cheese
5   ounces fresh mushrooms, sliced
36 slices Hormel® pepperoni
    Gluten-free flour for rolling pin

In a large nonstick skillet, heat 1 tablespoon olive oil over low heat. Add the garlic and cook, stirring frequently, about 2 minutes. Add tomatoes, oregano, and basil. Reduce heat and cook, stirring frequently until the tomato juices evaporate, about 10 minutes. Stir in tomato paste and cook for 2 minutes. Remove from heat; set aside.

Prepare pizza crust according to package directions. Oil one 14-inch perforated nonstick pizza pan. Roll dough into a ball; flatten and press into oiled pizza pan. Roll out into pan about ¼-inch thick using gluten-free floured rolling pin. Slightly raise dough around edges. Spread 1 tablespoon olive oil on crust and poke entire crust with a fork.

Bake pizza crust 10 minutes at 375°. Remove from oven and cool slightly. Use a large spoon to spread tomato sauce evenly over the surface of the prepared dough, within the rim. Cover the sauce with 1½ cups shredded mozzarella. Top with mushrooms and pepperoni slices. Sprinkle ½ cup mozzarella over the top. Place pizza in oven, and bake until the toppings are done, about 7 minutes.

Serves 3

Makes one 14-inch pizza. Mona's pizza mix may be ordered at www.madebymona.com or call (866) 486-0701 toll free. Really Great Food Company products may be ordered at www.reallygreatfood.com or call (800) 593-5377.

Sausage and Onion Pizza

3   Kinnikinnick 10-inch pizza crusts
¾   cup Contadina Pizza Squeeze pizza
     sauce
12   ounces (3 cups) Kraft shredded low-
     moisture part skim mozzarella
     cheese

8   ounces Johnsonville Italian ground
     sausage, cooked and drained
⅓   cup chopped onion
½   medium red bell pepper, cut into
     thin strips

Defrost pizza crust at room temperature for 10 minutes. Place on a 14-inch perforated nonstick pizza pan. Top with pizza sauce, mozzarella cheese, sausage, onion, and bell peppers.

Bake at 375° for 10 to 12 minutes until cheese is melted and lightly browned. Remove from oven and cool slightly.

Serves 4

Go to www.johnsonville.com (under FAQ) to confirm
gluten-free status of sausage. Kinnikinnick products can be ordered
at www.goglutenfree.com or call (877) 503-4466.

DESSERTS

Desserts

Banana Cake

Cake:

¼ cup (½ stick) butter, softened

2 cups Mona's Happy Day cake mix, divided

2 large eggs, at room temperature

2 medium ripe bananas, mashed

1 teaspoon McCormick pure vanilla extract

¼ teaspoon Calumet baking soda

2 tablespoons Breakstone's sour cream

Preheat the oven to 350°. Butter a 9 x 9-inch baking pan. In a large bowl of an electric mixer, cream butter. Add ½ cup cake mix and beat well. Add eggs, one at a time, beating well after each addition. Add banana and vanilla; beat on low speed for 30 seconds. Add remaining 1½ cup cake mix, baking soda, and sour cream. Beat well. Spoon into prepared pan and bake 25 to 30 minutes until light brown. Toothpick will come out clean when done. Remove from oven and let cool.

Frosting:

2 tablespoons butter, softened

1⅔ cups Domino® confectioners sugar

1-2 tablespoons milk

⅔ teaspoon McCormick pure vanilla extract

To prepare frosting, cream butter with an electric mixer. Gradually add confectioners sugar alternately with milk. Add vanilla extract and beat well. When cake has cooled, spread with the frosting.

Serves 12

Cake mix may be ordered at www.madebymona.com or call (866) 486-0701 toll free.

Birthday Cake

1   package (23 ounce) Really Great
    Food Company yellow cake mix
4   large eggs
1   cup milk
¾   cup butter, softened

1½ teaspoons McCormick pure vanilla
    extract
    Buttercream Frosting (recipe follows)
6   tablespoons seedless red raspberry
    preserves (such as Dickinson's)

Preheat oven to 375°. Grease two 8-inch round cake pans.

In a large bowl of an electric mixer, beat the butter until creamy, about 30 seconds. Gradually add the cake mix beating on low speed until combined. Scrape the sides of the bowl as necessary. Add eggs and beat. Slowly add milk and vanilla and blend to combine. Beat until creamy. Pour batter into 2 greased 8-inch round cake pans. Bake until a toothpick inserted in the center comes out clean, 30 to 35 minutes. Do not underbake.

Cool cake in pan 20 minutes. Run a sharp, thin knife around the edges of the cake to detach it from the pan. Place a wire rack over the top of the pan and invert the cake onto the rack. Turn right side up to cool completely.

Cut each cake layer into two layers lengthwise using a long bread knife. Place one layer, cut side down, onto serving plate and spread with 3 tablespoons raspberry jelly, spreading close to, but not up to the edges. Place next layer on top and spread with buttercream frosting. Place third layer on top and spread with remaining raspberry jelly. Place top layer on cake and spread tops and sides with buttercream frosting.

Serves 12

Really Great Food Company products may be ordered
at www.reallygreatfood.com or call (800) 593-5377.

Buttercream Frosting

½ cup (1 stick) butter, softened
1   pound Domino® confectioners sugar
     (3¾ cups)

2   teaspoons McCormick pure vanilla
     extract
3-4 tablespoons milk

In a large bowl of heavy-duty mixer, beat butter on low until fluffy. Add sugar, vanilla, and 3 tablespoons milk and blend until smooth. If necessary, add up to 1 tablespoon more milk until frosting is spreading consistency.

Serves 12

To make Chocolate Buttercream Frosting: Melt 1 square (1-ounce) unsweetened chocolate in microwave for 60 seconds. Stir to melt. Microwave for an additional 30 seconds if necessary. Stir chocolate into Buttercream Frosting.

Devil's Food Cake with Chocolate Frosting

Cake:

Crisco shortening for greasing the pans

Gluten-free flour for dusting the pans

4　large eggs

½　cup plus 1½ tablespoons vegetable oil

1　cup water

1　package (23 ounces) Really Great Food Company Devil's Food cake mix

Place oven rack in the center of the oven and preheat the oven to 350°. Generously grease and flour two 8-inch round cake pans. Shake out the excess flour and set aside.

Beat eggs with an electric mixer for 1 minute at medium speed. Add oil and water to eggs and beat again. Add the cake mix and blend on low speed for 1 minute. Stop the mixer and scrape down the sides of the bowl with a rubber spatula. Beat 1 minute more at medium speed. The batter should look well blended.

Pour the batter into the prepared pan and bake for about 40 to 48 minutes, until the cake springs back when lightly pressed with your finger. Cool on a wire rack for 10 minutes. Run a dinner knife around the edge of the pan and invert onto a rack and revert again so the cake is right side up. Allow to cool completely, about 45 minutes more.

Chocolate Sour Cream Frosting:

4　tablespoons (½ stick) butter, cut into 4 pieces

⅓　cup Hershey's Cocoa

1½ cups Domino® confectioners sugar, sifted

2　tablespoons Breakstone's sour cream

1　teaspoon McCormick pure vanilla extract

Microwave butter in a 2-cup glass measure on High (100% power) for 45 seconds. Add the cocoa and whisk until smooth. With an electric mixer on low speed, blend the butter mixture with the confectioners sugar alternately with the sour cream. Blend on low speed for 1 to 1½ minutes, or until incorporated. Stop the mixer and add the vanilla. Beat at medium speed until fluffy, about 1 minute more. Spread frosting over cooled cake. Place the cake, uncovered, in the refrigerator until the frosting sets, about 20 minutes. Store cake in the refrigerator.

Serves 12

Really Great Food Company products may be ordered at www.reallygreatfood.com or call (800) 593-5377.

Orange Cake

Cake:

Crisco shortening for greasing the pan

1 teaspoon gluten-free flour for dusting the pan

1 package 'Cause Your Special yellow cake mix

¼ cup Royal vanilla instant pudding & pie filling

½ cup orange juice (such as Tropicana Pure Premium)

¼ cup vegetable oil

2 tablespoons sugar

1 teaspoon McCormick pure vanilla extract

2 large eggs

Position oven rack in the center of the oven and preheat the oven to 350°. Lightly grease and flour a 8-inch round cake pan. Shake out the excess flour. Set aside.

In the large bowl of an electric mixer, beat the cake mix, pudding, orange juice, vegetable oil, sugar, vanilla, and eggs on low speed for 1 minute. Stop the mixer and scrape down the sides of the bowl with a rubber spatula. Increase the mixer speed to medium and beat for 2 minutes more, scraping down the sides of the bowl if needed. The batter should look thick and well blended. Pour the batter into the prepared pan and smooth with a spatula.

Bake 35 to 40 minutes, until the cake is golden brown and just starts to pull away from the sides of the pan. Cool on a wire rack for 20 minutes. Run a long sharp knife around the edge of the cake and invert it onto a rack to cool completely, about 30 minutes.

Frosting:

8 ounces Philadelphia cream cheese, softened

½ cup (1 stick) butter, softened

3 cups Domino® confectioners sugar, sifted

2 tablespoons orange juice (such as Tropicana Pure Premium)

1 tablespoon freshly grated orange peel (from 1 medium orange)

Place the cream cheese and butter in a large mixing bowl. Blend with an electric mixer on low speed until combined, 30 seconds. Stop the mixer and add the confectioners sugar, a bit at a time, blending with the mixer on low speed until the sugar is incorporated, about 1 minute. Add the orange juice and orange peel to the mixture. Beat at medium speed until the frosting lightens and is fluffy, about 1 minute more. Use at once to frost the top and sides of cake.

Serves 8

'Cause You're Special products may be ordered at www.causeyourespecial.com or call (866) 669-4328 toll free.

Cheesecake

Crust:

1	cup Kinnikinnick Graham Style Cracker Crumbs
2	tablespoons butter, melted
1	tablespoon sugar

Preheat oven to 350°. Lightly butter the sides and bottom of a 9-inch springform pan. Chill in refrigerator until ready to use. Blend graham cracker crumbs, melted butter, and sugar together in a small bowl. Press firmly onto bottom of springform pan.

Filling:

4	(8-ounce) packages Philadelphia cream cheese, softened
1	cup sugar
4	large eggs
1	teaspoon McCormick pure vanilla extract
2	tablespoons finely grated lemon peel (from 2 medium lemons)

In the bowl of an electric mixer, beat the cream cheese and sugar on low until smooth and fluffy. Add eggs, one at a time, and beat until well blended. Beat in vanilla and lemon peel. Pour filling over crust and bake until set, about 50 to 65 minutes. Run a knife or metal spatula around the rim of the pan to loosen cake; cool before removing rim of pan.

Topping:

1   can (21 ounces) Lucky Leaf cherry pie filling

Completely cover top of cake with cherry pie filling. Refrigerate 2 to 4 hours, or overnight.

Serves 12

Kinnikinnick products may be ordered
at www.goglutenfree.com or call (877) 503-4466.

Strawberry Cheesecake

Crust: ✓

1½ cups Kinnikinnick Graham Style
    Cracker Crumbs

¼ cup sugar
¼ cup (½ stick) butter, melted

Preheat oven to 375°. Mix cracker crumbs, sugar, and butter until well blended. Press firmly on bottom and up side of 9-inch pie plate. Bake 8 minutes or until lightly browned. Transfer to rack and cool while preparing filling.

Filling:

2 (8-ounce) packages Philadelphia
    cream cheese, softened
½ cup sugar

2 large eggs
½ teaspoon McCormick pure vanilla
    extract

Beat cream cheese and sugar with electric mixer on medium speed until well blended. Add eggs and vanilla and blend. Pour into prepared 9-inch crust. Bake at 350° for 40 minutes or until center is almost set. Cool. Refrigerate 3 hours or overnight.

Topping:

2 ounces Cool Whip®, thawed

8 ounces strawberries, halved

Spread Cool Whip over cheesecake. Arrange strawberries on top of cheesecake. Store leftover cheesecake in the refrigerator.

Serves 8

Kinnikinnick products may be ordered
at www.goglutenfree.com or call (877) 503-4466.

Strawberry Shortcake

16 ounces strawberries, sliced

1 tablespoon Domino® confectioners sugar

1 teaspoon unsalted butter, at room temperature, for greasing the pan

¾ cup butter, softened

4 large eggs

1 (19.5 ounce) package 'Cause Your Special golden pound cake mix

Reddi-wip® Original whipped light cream

Combine sliced strawberries and confectioners sugar in a bowl; stir well. Cover and chill 2 hours.

Preheat oven to 350°. Butter a 10 x 5-inch loaf pan.

In the bowl of an electric mixer fitted with the paddle attachment, cream butter at medium speed until light, pale, and fluffy. Add eggs and blend at medium speed, scraping down the sides of the bowl as necessary. Gradually add cake mix, beating until dry ingredients are completely moistened (about 3 minutes). Using a large rubber spatula, scrape the batter into the prepared pan.

Bake at 350° for 60 to 70 minutes or until a wooden pick inserted in center comes out clean. Cool the cake in the pan on a wire rack for 20 minutes, then invert onto the rack and cool completely. Slice pound cake into 1-inch slices and place each slice on a serving plate or shallow bowl. Top each cake slice with strawberries and some of the juice. Top with Reddi-wip.

Serves 10

'Cause You're Special products may be ordered at www.causeyourespecial.com or call (866) 669-4328 toll free.

Apple Crisp

4 whole Granny Smith apples, peeled and sliced
½ teaspoon cinnamon (such as McCormick)
3 tablespoons sugar

⅓ cup Bob's Red Mill sorghum flour
1 tablespoon cornstarch (such as Argo)
⅛ teaspoon salt
2 tablespoons butter, melted

Preheat oven to 350°. Place the apple slices in an 8 x 8-inch glass baking dish and sprinkle with cinnamon. In a small bowl, mix sugar, sorghum flour, cornstarch, and salt. Add melted butter and stir. Sprinkle crumble topping over apples. Bake until bubbly and golden brown. Let stand for 15 minutes. Serve warm with ice cream.

Serves 4

Bob's Red Mill flour may be ordered at www.bobsredmill.com or call (800) 349-2173.

Chocolate Crispy Bars

3 tablespoons butter
1 package (10 ounces) marshmallows
   (such as Jet-Puffed)

6 cups EnviroKidz Organic Koala
   Crisp cereal

Melt butter in a large saucepan over low heat. Add marshmallows and stir until completely melted. Remove from heat. Immediately add cereal and stir until well coated. Using waxed paper, press mixture evenly into a greased 13 x 9-inch pan. Cut into 2-inch squares when cool.

Microwave directions: In a microwave safe bowl, heat butter and marshmallows on high for 2 minutes. Stir until smooth. Microwave 1 minute more; stir. Immediately add cereal and stir until well coated. Using waxed paper, press mixture evenly into a greased 13 x 9-inch pan. Cut into 2-inch squares when cool.

Serves 24

These bars are best served on the same day they are prepared.

Pumpkin Bars

Pumpkin Bars:

¾ cup Bob's Red Mill white rice flour
⅔ cup Bob's Red Mill potato starch
⅓ cup Bob's Red Mill tapioca flour
2 tablespoons Bob's Red Mill
   sorghum flour
1 tablespoon McCormick cinnamon
2 teaspoons Rumford baking powder
1 teaspoon Calumet baking soda

½ teaspoon salt
¼ teaspoon McCormick ground ginger
½ teaspoon McCormick ground cloves
4 large eggs, at room temperature
1 can (15 ounce) Libby's 100% Pure
   Pumpkin
2 cups sugar
¾ cup vegetable oil

Preheat oven to 350°. Grease a 15 x 10 x 1-inch baking pan. Mix flours, cinnamon, baking powder, baking soda, salt, ginger, and cloves together with a whisk; set aside. In the large bowl of an electric mixer, beat eggs for 1 minute on medium speed. Add pumpkin, sugar, and vegetable oil and beat until blended. Add flour mixture and blend until smooth. Spread batter into prepared pan. Bake 20 to 25 minutes or until a toothpick inserted in center comes out clean. Cool in pan on rack.

frosting:

8 ounces Philadelphia cream cheese
6 tablespoons butter

2 teaspoons McCormick pure vanilla
   extract
3 cups Domino® confectioners sugar

Soften cream cheese and butter in microwave on High (100% power) for 12 seconds each. Beat cream cheese and butter in electric mixer; add vanilla. Gradually add the confectioners sugar. Beat until well blended. Spread frosting over cooled cake. Cut into bars and serve.

Serves 24

Mark is the dessert specialist in our family. This is the
dessert he asks for most. I can't think of a higher recommendation!

Brownie Cupcakes

1¼ cups Nestle semisweet chocolate chips

3 ounces Nestle unsweetened chocolate

6 tablespoons unsalted butter, cut into 4 pieces

½ cup Domino® light brown sugar

⅓ cup sugar

2 large eggs

1 teaspoon McCormick pure vanilla extract

¼ cup Bob's Red Mill tapioca flour

¼ cup Bob's Red Mill sorghum flour

⅓ cup walnuts, chopped

¼ teaspoon salt

Preheat oven to 350°. Line 12 muffin cups with paper liners.

Microwave ½ cup chocolate chips, unsweetened chocolate, and butter in a microwave-safe glass mixing bowl on medium (50% power) for 1 minute. Heat for additional 30 second increments until only a few lumps of chocolate remain. Whisk until chocolate is melted and smooth.

Whisk both sugars into the chocolate mixture, then mix in eggs one at a time. Whisk in vanilla, then flour. Stir in walnuts, salt, and remaining ¾ cup chocolate chips. Divide batter among prepared muffin cups. Bake cupcakes until tester inserted into center comes out with moist crumbs attached, about 20 minutes. Turn cupcakes onto a rack to cool completely.

Serves 12

Bob's Red Mill flour may be ordered at www.bobsredmill.com or call (800) 349-2173.

Turtle Brownies

Brownie Layer:

Bob's Red Mill gluten free brownie mix

¾ cup (1½ sticks) butter, melted

1 egg

2 teaspoons McCormick pure vanilla extract

¾ cup warm (110°) water

Preheat oven to 350°. Butter a 9 x 13-inch metal baking pan. Prepare brownies according to package directions. Do not add chocolate chips to batter.

Caramel-Pecan Layer:

1¼ cups sugar

½ cup Karo light corn syrup

⅓ cup water

½ cup heavy cream

2 teaspoons McCormick pure vanilla extract

16 ounces pecans (3 cups)

Pinch of salt

Bring sugar, corn syrup, water, and pinch of salt to a boil in a 3-quart heavy saucepan over moderate heat, stirring until the sugar is dissolved. Boil, without stirring, until mixture turns a golden caramel color, about 10 minutes. Remove from heat and carefully add cream and vanilla (mixture will bubble and steam). Stir in pecans and immediately pour over brownie layer, spreading evenly. Cool completely in pan on rack.

Garnish:

3 ounces Baker's semisweet chocolate, melted

Melt chocolate in microwave for 30 seconds on high. Repeat for 30 second intervals until chocolate begins to melt. Stir with wooden spoon until melted. Spoon chocolate into a small Ziploc bag and seal, forcing out excess air. Squeeze chocolate into one corner, then cut a tiny slice off corner to form a small hole. Squeeze chocolate decoratively over brownies.

Chill brownies, loosely covered, until caramel and chocolate are firm, at least 4 hours. Just before serving, cut chilled brownies into 36 squares and remove from pan while still cold, then bring to room temperature before serving. Serve with vanilla ice cream.

Serves 36

Bob's Red Mill Gluten Free Brownie Mix is sold
at natural foods stores and some supermarkets. Brownie mix may
also be ordered at www.bobsredmill.com or call (800) 349-2173.

Nursery School Cookies

24 Hershey's Kisses Brand Milk
   Chocolates
1 cup sugar

1 cup peanut butter (such as Jif)
1 medium egg, beaten

Put oven rack in middle position and preheat oven to 350°. Remove wrappers from chocolates. Beat sugar and peanut butter in a large mixing bowl until combined. Add egg and mix well. Form into small balls using a small cookie scoop. Place 2 inches apart on ungreased baking sheet.

Bake 10 minutes. Remove from oven. Place a chocolate kiss in the center of each cookie, pressing down gently so cookie cracks around the edges. Bake additional 1 minute. Let cool on baking sheet for 2 minutes, then transfer to a wire cooling rack with a spatula.

Serves 12

I admit I was a bit skeptical when I got this cookie recipe from
my friend because the ingredients are so simple. These are really great cookies
and so easy to make. As you might expect, they are a bit sweet.

Peanut Butter Chocolate Chip Cookies

½ cup (1 stick) butter, softened
¾ cup creamy peanut butter (such as Simply Jif)
1 large egg
1 cup Bob's Red Mill white rice flour
¼ cup Bob's Red Mill tapioca flour

½ cup sugar
½ cup Domino® light brown sugar
½ teaspoon Calumet baking soda
½ teaspoon Rumford baking powder
2 cups (12-ounce package) Nestle Toll House semi-sweet chocolate morsels

Preheat oven to 375°. In a large bowl, beat butter and peanut butter with an electric mixer until well blended. Add egg, flours, sugars, baking soda, and baking powder. Beat until thoroughly combined. Add in chocolate morsels and mix with a large spoon. Shape into 1-inch balls, and flatten by crisscrossing with a fork. Bake until lightly browned, about 8 minutes.

Serves 24

Bob's Red Mill flour may be ordered
at www.bobsredmill.com or call (800) 349-2173.

Vegan Chocolate Chip Cookies

1½ cups Mona's Multi Mix
½ teaspoon Calumet baking soda
¼ teaspoon salt
¼ cup soy milk (such as Silk)
1 tablespoon Bob's Red Mill flaxseed meal
¼ cup Domino® light brown sugar

½ cup sugar
⅓ cup canola oil
2 teaspoons McCormick pure vanilla extract
¾ cup vegan chocolate chips (such as Tropical Source)

Preheat oven to 350°. Line two baking sheets with parchment paper. In a small mixing bowl, whisk together Mona's Mix, baking soda, and salt. Set aside.

In the large bowl of an electric mixer, beat soy milk, flaxseed meal, sugar, oil, and vanilla on low until light and fluffy, about 2 minutes. Gradually add reserved dry ingredients and mix until well blended. Mix in chocolate chips.

Using a small cookie scoop, shape into 1-inch balls, and place on baking sheets. Using waxed paper, flatten each ball to a 2-inch round. Bake until lightly browned, about 10 to 12 minutes. Remove from oven and cool on baking sheet for 2 minutes. Transfer cookies to racks and cool completely.

Serves 12

A vegan diet consists of plant-based foods, such as fruits, vegetables, whole grains, legumes, nuts, and seeds. The vegan diet eliminates all foods from animals (meat, poultry, and fish). Dairy products are also excluded (eggs, milk, cheese, and butter).

Andrew's Brownie Sundae

1   Mr. Ritt's chocolate brownie
3   scoops Edy's Grand Vanilla Bean ice
    cream

2   tablespoons Smucker's hot fudge
    topping
    Reddi-wip® Original whipped light
    cream

Place brownie in the bottom of an ice cream bowl. Add vanilla ice cream and top with hot fudge. Add Reddi-wip topping and serve.

Serves 1

Gluten-free brownies can be ordered from
Mr. Ritt's bakery in Philadelphia. Call (215) 627-3034.

Banana Split

1 medium ripe banana

3 scoops Edy's Grand ice cream, Vanilla Bean, Strawberry, and Chocolate

1 tablespoon Smucker's chocolate sauce

1 tablespoon Smucker's butterscotch sauce

1 tablespoon Smucker's strawberry sauce

Reddi-wip® Original Whipped Light Cream

1 tablespoon chopped walnuts or pecans

2 maraschino cherries

Cut the banana in half lengthwise and put it in a long, shallow glass dish. Place ice cream scoops along the length of the banana, between the two halves. Drizzle the 3 sauces over the top. Add Reddi-wip around the base of the dish and over the ice cream. Sprinkle with chopped nuts and top with cherries.

Serves 1

Ginger and Peach Ice Cream Cake

1   package (125 grams) Glutano Ginger Cookies, crushed in blender

½   cup slivered almonds, toasted and chopped in blender

2   teaspoons unsalted butter, melted and cooled

1   tablespoon Karo light corn syrup

1   cup Hagen-Dazs Orchard Peach Sorbet

1   cup vanilla ice cream (such as Edy's or Dryer's)

Line a 3½ x 7½-inch loaf pan with a double layer of plastic wrap, allowing a few inches overhang along sides. Stir together cookie crumbs, almonds, butter, and corn syrup in a small bowl, then press into bottom of loaf pan.

Soften sorbet in microwave for 10 seconds. Spread sorbet evenly over crumb crust and freeze 30 minutes to harden. While sorbet is freezing, slightly soften ice cream. Spread evenly over sorbet and freeze, covered with plastic wrap, until firm, at least 2 hours.

Using plastic wrap as an aid, lift frozen cake out of pan, then peel off plastic. Let stand 5 minutes to soften, then cut crosswise into 4 slices.

Serves 4

Toasting nuts brings out their flavor. To toast almonds, spread nuts in a single layer in a shallow baking pan. Toast in a 350° oven until golden brown, 3 to 5 minutes.

Nana's Hot Fudge Sundae

3   scoops Dairy Queen vanilla ice
     cream, packed in a quart container
2   tablespoons Smucker's hot fudge
     topping

2   tablespoons pecan halves
     Reddi-wip® Original whipped light
     cream

Heat hot fudge topping in jar in microwave on high heat for 30 seconds. Scoop two scoops of ice cream into a sundae glass and top with 1 tablespoon hot fudge topping. Sprinkle with pecans. Add the remaining scoop of ice cream and spoon the remaining hot fudge over the top. Add the Reddi-wip and serve.

Serves 1

Strawberry Sundaes

8   ounces fresh strawberries
1   tablespoon Domino® confectioners
     sugar

8   scoops Edy's Grand (or Dreyer's)
     Real Strawberry ice cream
     Reddi-wip® Original whipped light
     cream

Rinse the strawberries and pat dry with paper towels. Hull and halve the strawberries and place in a bowl. Sprinkle with confectioners sugar, and set aside for 30 minutes. Scoop one scoop of ice cream into 4 sundae dishes and top with berries. Add another scoop of ice cream and top with berries and Reddi-wip topping.

Serves 4

HOLIDAYS

Holidays

Spinach and Avocado Salad

½ cup olive oil
¼ cup Regina red wine vinegar
1 teaspoon McCormick basil leaves
2 cloves garlic, chopped
2 teaspoons sugar
7 ounces baby spinach leaves

1 medium red onion, very thinly
    sliced
1 cup walnuts
2 medium avocados, sliced
    Salt and freshly ground black pepper

Whisk oil, vinegar, basil, garlic, and sugar in a small bowl until sugar dissolves. Season dressing with salt and pepper. Mix spinach, red onion, and walnuts in a large serving bowl. Add avocados and dressing. Toss gently to coat.

Serves 12

Call (888) 887-3266 to confirm gluten-free status of Regina red wine vinegar.

Orange and Maple Roasted Turkey

Turkey:

¾ cup orange juice

¼ cup pure maple syrup

1 fresh turkey (about 12 pounds)

1 tablespoon freshly grated orange peel

¼ teaspoon salt

¼ teaspoon pepper

1 medium orange, quartered

1 medium onion, quartered

Position rack in bottom third of oven; preheat to 375°. Combine orange juice and syrup in a small saucepan; bring just to a boil. Remove from heat; set aside.

Remove giblets (including liver) and neck from turkey, and set aside. Rinse turkey thoroughly with cold water, and pat dry with paper towels. Sprinkle grated orange peel, salt, and pepper into the body cavity and onto the bird. Stuff cavity of turkey with orange quarters and onion quarters. Tie legs together with kitchen string.

Place the turkey, breast-side up, on a rack in a roasting pan. Insert meat thermometer into meaty part of thigh, making sure not to touch bone. Bake the turkey at 375° for 45 minutes.

Baste turkey with the orange juice mixture; cover turkey loosely with foil. Bake turkey an additional 2 hours and 15 minutes or until the thermometer registers 180°, or until juices run clear when thickest part of thigh is pierced with skewer, basting turkey every 30 minutes. Let turkey stand for 10 minutes; set the pan and drippings aside to make gravy.

Gravy:

1 teaspoon butter

Neck and giblets (excluding liver) from turkey

2 cups water

4 cups Kitchen Basics chicken stock

1 celery rib, coarsely chopped

1 medium carrot, coarsely chopped

1 medium onion, coarsely chopped

1 bay leaf

1 tablespoon pure maple syrup

¼ teaspoon freshly grated orange peel

2 tablespoons orange juice

2 tablespoons cornstarch (such as Argo)

Salt and freshly ground black pepper

Melt butter in a medium saucepan over medium heat. Add giblets and neck; cook and stir 2 minutes or until browned on all sides. Add water, chicken stock, celery, carrot, and onion. Bring to a boil; skim froth. Add bay leaf and cover. Reduce heat and simmer 1 to 2 hours.

Remove giblets and neck from stock mixture and discard. Straddle roasting pan across 2 burners, then pour stock through a sieve into roasting pan. Deglaze pan by boiling over high heat, stirring and scraping up brown bits, about 1 minute. Pour through fine-mesh sieve into a bowl; discard solids. Remove fat from surface with a spoon.

Transfer the stock mixture to a saucepan; add syrup and orange peel. In a small bowl, whisk orange juice and cornstarch until cornstarch is dissolved. Add to stock mixture and whisk until well-blended. Bring to a boil; cook 1 minute or until thick. Season with salt and pepper. Serve gravy with turkey.

Serves 8

Baked Ham

1 **(3 pound) Dietz & Watson Tiffany boneless ham (or Hormel Cure 81 ham)**	3 **tablespoons orange juice (such as Tropicana Pure Premium)**
½ **cup Domino® light brown sugar**	1 **teaspoon McCormick ground mustard**
2 **tablespoons honey**	24 **McCormick whole cloves**

Preheat oven to 350°. Place the ham in a shallow baking dish. Insert a meat thermometer into center of ham. Bake the ham unglazed for 20 minutes.

Prepare ham for glazing by scoring the outside in a diamond pattern, cutting ¼-inch deep with a sharp knife. Combine the brown sugar, honey, orange juice, and mustard in a small bowl. Mix well and spread some of the glaze over the outside of the ham. Stud with whole cloves in the center of each diamond.

Return the ham to the oven to finish baking, brushing with glaze every 20 minutes. Cook ham until the internal temperature is 140° to warm the meat and melt the glaze, about 1 hour. Let ham rest 10 minutes before carving.

Serves 8

Please go to the FAQs at www.dietzandwatson.com
or www.hormel.com to confirm the gluten-free status of ham.

Rice Dressing

3	cups cooked rice	2	tablespoons McCormick parsley flakes
½	pound Oscar Mayer bacon, cut in 2-inch strips	1	cup Kitchen Basics chicken stock
2	medium onions, chopped	3	tablespoons butter, melted
1	cup chopped celery (4-6 ribs)		Salt and freshly ground black pepper

Preheat oven to 375°. Cook bacon in a large nonstick skillet over medium-low heat until crisp. Transfer to paper towels and drain. Crumble bacon and set aside. Wipe skillet clean leaving 1 tablespoon bacon fat. Cook onions and celery in bacon fat until softened, about 2 minutes.

In a large bowl, combine rice, bacon, onions, celery, and parsley. Season with salt and freshly ground black pepper. Drizzle dressing with chicken stock and melted butter. Spoon into a 3-4 quart buttered baking dish. Bake, covered, 20 minutes; then uncover and bake an additional 20 minutes until dressing is heated through.

Serves 8

Cranberry Orange Relish

6	navel oranges	½	cup freshly squeezed orange juice
1	cup sugar	16	ounces fresh cranberries
1	cup water	2	teaspoons finely grated orange peel

Cut away and discard peel and pith from oranges, then cut sections free from membranes. Place sugar, water, and orange juice in a medium saucepan over medium heat. Cook and stir until sugar dissolves, about 5 minutes. Add cranberries and simmer just until berries start to pop, about 10 minutes. Remove from heat, and stir in orange peel and orange sections. Cool completely at room temperature. Refrigerate overnight.

Serves 10

This sauce must be made 1 to 3 days in
advance of serving to allow the flavors to mellow.

Green Beans with Bacon

2½ pounds green beans, trimmed
8 slices Oscar Mayer bacon, cut in half

3 tablespoons butter
4 large shallots, finely chopped

Cook green beans in boiling water for 3 minutes. Drain and rinse under cold water. Wrap in paper towels, and place in a Ziploc bag. Can be refrigerated up to 6 hours ahead. Cook bacon in large skillet over medium heat until crisp. Remove from skillet and drain on paper towels. Discard all but 3 tablespoons bacon fat from skillet. Add butter to skillet and melt over medium heat. Add shallots and cook and stir 2 minutes. Add beans and cook, stirring occasionally, until heated thorough, about 6 minutes. Crumble bacon and add to beans. Toss to blend. Season with salt and pepper.

Serves 8

Cheesy Potatoes

6   medium new potatoes
8   ounces Cheddar cheese (such as
    Heluva® Good), sliced
¼   cup (½ stick) butter

¾   cup Breakstone's sour cream
⅓   cup chopped sweet onion
    Salt and freshly ground black pepper

Boil potatoes in skins until tender, 15 to 25 minutes depending on size. Peel and shred coarsely. In saucepan, over low heat, combine cheese and butter. Stir until melted. Remove from heat and add sour cream and onion. Fold sauce into potatoes. Spread into greased 11 x 8 x 3-inch baking pan and season with salt and pepper. Bake, uncovered, at 350° for 30 minutes or until bubbly throughout.

Serves 6

Maple Mashed Sweet Potatoes

6   pounds sweet potatoes
½   cup (1 stick) unsalted butter, melted
½   cup heavy cream, warmed

2   tablespoons pure maple syrup
1   teaspoon salt
    Freshly ground black pepper

Position rack in bottom third of oven; preheat to 400°. Prick each potato twice with a fork and bake in a foil-lined shallow baking pan until very tender, about 1 hour. Remove and cool slightly. Halve potatoes lengthwise and carefully scoop pulp into a large bowl. Mash potatoes with a potato masher or, for a smoother purée, force through a potato ricer. Stir in butter, cream, and syrup. Season with salt and pepper.

Serves 10

Pumpkin Pie

Pie Crust:

1   package (125 grams) Glutano ginger   2½ tablespoons butter, melted
    cookies (1½ cups)   2   tablespoons sugar

Place ginger cookies in a one gallon Ziploc bag. Seal and crush cookies with a rolling pin. Combine crushed cookies, butter, and sugar in a bowl and toss with a fork until moist. Press into bottom and ½ way up sides of a 9-inch pie plate.

Filling:

¾ cup sugar   2   large eggs
1   teaspoon McCormick cinnamon   15 ounces Libby's 100% Pure
½ teaspoon salt   Pumpkin
½ teaspoon McCormick ground ginger   1   (12-ounce) can Carnation
¼ teaspoon McCormick ground cloves   evaporated milk

Preheat oven to 350°.

Combine sugar, cinnamon, salt, ginger, and cloves in a small bowl. Set aside. Beat eggs in a large bowl. Stir in pumpkin and sugar-spice mixture. Gradually stir in evaporated milk. Pour into prepared crust. Cover crust with pie crust shield to avoid burning. Bake at 350° for 60 to 70 minutes or until a knife inserted in center comes out clean. Cool on a wire rack for 2 hours. Serve immediately or refrigerate

Serves 8

Glutano cookies may be ordered at www.glutenfreemall.com.

Mashed Potato Casserole

5   large baking potatoes, cut into
    1-inch slices
1   (4-ounce) package Philadelphia
    cream cheese, softened
1   cup Breakstone's sour cream

1   envelope Good Seasons Italian Salad
    Dressing & Recipe Mix
½   cup (1 stick) butter, softened
1   cup milk
    McCormick paprika

Grease a 13 x 9-inch baking dish. Place potatoes in a saucepan; add water to cover, and bring to a boil. Cover, reduce heat, and simmer 20 minutes or until very tender; drain and mash coarsely. Add the cream cheese, sour cream, dressing mix, and butter. Add the milk, a little at a time, until the desired consistency is reached. Spread mixture into prepared baking dish and sprinkle with paprika. Cover and refrigerate overnight or up to 24 hours. Bake, covered with foil, at 325° for 25 to 30 minutes.

Serves 8

Pop Pop's Fudge

Fudge:

3 cups milk

6 squares Baker's semi-sweet chocolate

6 cups sugar

6 Tablespoons Karo® light corn syrup
   Dash salt (less than ⅛ teaspoon)

¼ cup (½ stick) butter

1 tablespoon McCormick pure vanilla extract

2 cups coarsely chopped pecans (optional)

Special equipment:

Clip-on candy thermometer

Lightly butter a 13 x 9 x 2-inch baking pan. Combine milk and chocolate in a deep (8-inch) heavy-bottomed saucepan over medium heat. Cook until chocolate is melted and mixture thickens, stirring with a wooden spoon.

Add sugar, corn syrup, and salt. Stir until sugar dissolves and mixture begins to boil. Attach clip-on candy thermometer to side of pan. Cook, stirring constantly, until temperature registers 234° (soft ball stage), about 10 minutes. Mixture will bubble up. Remove the pan from the heat and add the butter.

Stir vigorously with a wooden spoon until the temperature has lowered to 150°, 15 to 20 minutes. Add vanilla and beat with a wooden spoon until the chocolate mixture begins to lose its gloss, about 1 to 2 minutes (no less than 140°). Add nuts, if desired, and quickly spread into prepared pan. When firm, cut into squares.

Serves 36

My dad makes this old-fashioned fudge for family holidays.
It's really tasty and we all love it!

Table of Equivalents

1 tablespoon	=	3 teaspoons
¼ cup	=	4 tablespoons
⅓ cup	=	5 tablespoons plus 1 teaspoon
½ cup	=	8 tablespoons
⅔ cup	=	10 tablespoons plus 2 teaspoons
¾ cup	=	12 tablespoons
1 cup	=	16 tablespoons
1 cup	=	8 fluid ounces
1 cup	=	½ pint
1 pint	=	2 cups
1 quart	=	2 pints (or 4 cups)
1 gallon	=	4 quarts (or 16 cups)

To divide a recipe in half:

Whole Recipe	Half-Recipe
1 tablespoon	1½ teaspoons
3 tablespoons	1½ tablespoons (or 1 tablespoon plus 1½ teaspoons)
¼ cup	2 tablespoons
⅓ cup	2 tablespoons plus 2 teaspoons
½ cup	¼ cup
⅔ cup	⅓ cup
¾ cup	¼ cup plus 2 tablespoons
1 cup	½ cup
1 pint	1 cup
1 quart	2 cups
1 egg	Beat the egg so the yolk and white are well mixed, let the bubbles settle, and measure 2 tablespoons (½ egg).

Susan Cornelius Hinderaker

Susan is a landscape designer and cookbook publisher. She graduated from the University of Chicago in 1981. She lives in Weddington, North Carolina with her husband, James, and two children, Andrew and Mark.

Andrew Hinderaker

Andrew is a senior at Charlotte Latin School in Charlotte, NC where he is currently preparing for college and developing his photography portfolio. His work has appeared in the school newspaper, The Hawkeye, the yearbook, Eyry, and the art and literary magazine, The Blue Review.

Notes

Index

C